WANDERINGS THROUGH THE GARHWAL HIMALAYA

WANDERINGS THROUGH THE GARHWAL HIMALAYA

GANESH SAILI

NIYOGI BOOKS

Published by
NIYOGI BOOKS
Block D, Building No. 77,
Okhla Industrial Area, Phase-I,
New Delhi-110 020, INDIA
Tel: 91-11-26816301, 26818960
Email: niyogibooks@gmail.com
Website: www.niyogibooksindia.com

Editor: Upama Biswas
Design: PealiDezine

ISBN: 978-93-85285-32-5
Publication: 2017
Reprint: 2025

Printed at: Niyogi Offset Pvt. Ltd., New Delhi, India.

To the memory of my grandfather
Govind Ram Saili,
who took me by the hand
on my first few steps
in Garhwal.

Contents

Introduction 08

Himalayan Magic 18

Glorious Garhwal 38

Trekking the Garhwals 44

Not So Quiet Flows the Yamuna 60

Travels With the Four-Horned Ram 70

The Man Who Would be King 78

The Magic of Duirital 86

Chandrashila 92

Baadis: The Flower Children of Garhwal 98

Travels in the Bhyundar Valley 104

Haridwar: Along the Ganga 114

Himalayan Blossoms	124
Other Denizens of Garhwal	134
Great Spirits of the Himalaya	148
Dharali: A Place for All Reasons	156
A Return to Uttarkashi	162
Where Rivers Run Deep	170
Mana's Mystic Magic	184
Looking Down at the Doon	190
Wanderings Around a Hill Station	206
A Tour in the Hills	216
Along the Road to Tehri	230
Index	239

A rare image of Badri Bugyal ©TS Chauhan

Introduction

Tungnath is the highest of the Panch Kedar, just a little way below Chandrashila peak

The night does indeed have 'a thousand eyes' if you were to look down at the valley below from our little perch in the foothills. But I must look northwards where looms large the mountains of Garhwal. Out here came my father, as a sixteen-year-old, with little more than his dreams. He had joined the male exodus from our village in the remote hills of Chamoli, in search of any job that would give him some money.

If time travel were possible, you would have found a strapping lad, with little baggage other than his dreams, undecided what to do or where to go next.

'I had no money, so I stood at the Rishikesh bus stand,' he would tell us years later. 'I looked at the charts for the cheapest ticket. Threw the dice and the one to these foothills won the cosmic lottery!'

Years later, I too set out on a walkabout. But mine was a journey of going back to the very mountains he had struggled to get away from. Mine was a journey in search of my roots. So, gentle reader, this clutch of essays, written over a period of forty years, are simply straws in the wind, or plain tales of travels, or wanderings through the enchanted valleys. To say: 'I am held hostage!' would be an understatement.

I began in the valley of the Doon where the Great Trignometrical Survey of India was set up; where in the 1860s, Colonel Montgomerie trained his handpicked native explorers in ingenious secret surveying techniques and then unleashed them into forbidden and hitherto unmapped parts of Central Asia. In these workshops were crafted 'special' Buddhist prayer wheels, pilgrims' staves to conceal compasses, notebooks and thermometers. The old

pundits' haunts evoke memories of Nain Singh, Kishen Singh and Kintup, those remarkable men who risked their lives in unchartered lands on the 'Roof of the World'.

Like those explorers, I too found in Garhwal, a place where every little nook and cranny, cave, rivulet or brook, is dedicated to some sage or saint, who happened to be fond of the area. I too worked my

When the mountain beckons, everything else, other than camping in the great outdoors, is a remote second

way through the travelogues of Rahul Sankrityayan, Kaka Sahib Kalelkar, Dr Govind Chatak and Vidyasagar Nautiyal.

In the ancient city of Haridwar, in a second-hand shop, I found a tattered copy of *La Prima Catholica Net Tibet* as also another book by Wessels, *Early Jesuit Travellers in Central Asia*. In these books I discovered the name of Father Antonio de Andrade, a Jesuit monk, who was the first European to enter Garhwal in 1624, having arrived in Goa in 1600.

I went past Adi Badri to Gairsain, home to the legendary Chander Singh Garhwali (who refused to open fire on unarmed civilians during the freedom struggle) and on to Ranikhet to meet the legendary Thakur Surbir Singh of the

On the edges of a glacial lake are the shrines of Lokpal and Hemkund

Tehri Durbar if only to get a glimpse of his personal library. Just my bad luck that the crumbling parchment scrolls were in Prakrit!

So I turned back to the Bhagirathi valley where I saw the nineteenth century mansion of the English freebooter Pahari Wilson. It has withstood the ravages of Time. Of course, he too did a bit of writing, but it is eminently forgettable. Posterity remembers him for everything else but his writing: entrepreneur, shikari, logger and raconteur, who plundered our forests.

It was here in Harsil, I remember a cavalcade of official vehicles with lights flashing and siren's blaring. They jarred the senses.

'There they go back to the plains. There goes your dreams of a Himalayan state. You'd be lucky to even get a belch out of them!' mutters an old-timer.

True! For people like him, little has changed. Angry mountain torrents are still crossed as they were two hundred years ago when a Lt. White recorded: 'The sangas were rudimentary – just bare tree trunks thrown across the waters. You've got

to clamber like monkeys where the side-rails are considered superfluous.'

It was Baille Fraser, an accomplished amateur artist in India in the first quarter of the nineteenth century, who gave us our first sketch of Gangotri in 1815, printed in *Views of the Himachal Mountains* in 1820. Following him, forty years later came Simpson, a professional landscape artist. He stayed in India between 1859 and 1862, resurrecting this very same scene. In the course of his travels he visited the Gaumukh glacier, the source of the Ganga. In typical understatement he says: 'I had my morning dip below the glacier, and I drank a little water.'

Above the waters of the Alaknanda river in Srinagar-Garhwal was an old bridge painted by Daniels, Thomas and William, in 1789. No trace remains today but when they arrived here with an escort of fifty sepoys, they found the bridge of ropes crammed with folks fleeing in panic with pots and pans from a pursuing army.

Oh! One can understand their relief and wash of nostalgia as they found the old familiars of

England: fir trees, wormwood, wild cherries, yellow raspberries and even the stinging nettle!

'Down-to-the-river and up-the-opposite-hill' they waded through crowds of curious locals who had never set their eyes on a white person before. Raja Praduman Shah was presented a watch and a pair of pistols.

But the artists did not stay back to get involved in a local skirmish. Soon after, in 1796 came Thomas Hardwicke, a soldier, zoologist and botanist to whom we owe the first images of the Himalayan rhododendrons. Though the flowering *mandar* or the magnolia here were a favourite of the seventeenth century painter-poet Mola Ram, you will not find a single of his miniatures here. They have gone the way of commerce. But despair not, staying here till eternity, in the sands of the river are the half-buried temples of a bygone age.

During this period, Shyam Shah ruled Garhwal. He was a liberal ruler but an impatient man, who ordered the disarming of some Naga sadhus who insisted on taking their weapons with them after finishing their stint at the Kumbh Mela and were going on a pilgrimage to Badrinath. On their refusal to comply, he asked his troops to expel them from his state.

The Ganga breaks free of the mountains at Rishikesh to begin its long journey to the Bay of Bengal

Though for E.T. Atkinson there was no turning back, as the *Himalayan Gazetteer* remains a ready reckoner. It never ceases to amaze me that how little we know about the man behind the work. He was the atypical self-effacing civil servant from the Raj where one was judged solely by one's work.

Cut from the same matrix came G.R.C. William, whose imperishable record of the Battle of Nalapani gives us a vivid account of both the victor and the vanquished: the British and the Gurkhas. A raucous meeting that marks the beginning of the arrival of the Raj into Garhwal. Whereafter, the portions that lay to the west of the Alaknanda were restored to the Garhwal Raja, while the victors took the spoils.

Other victors from the First War live on today—at least their names do—in windswept Chamba, along the road to Tehri, once home to Naik Darwan Singh Negi, a rifleman decorated with the Victoria Cross.

A military band plays at the closing of the portals of the Badrinath shrine in winter

One cannot hope to go past Tehri without remembering the valiant martyr Sridev Suman who joined the blazed a trail into history with an eighty-four day hunger strike. Nor can you ignore the drums at Maletha evoking memories of the warrior Madho Singh Bhandari: '*Ek singh ran koh/ ek singh bann koh, ek singh Madho Singh/ Aur singh kai koh?*' (One lion to the battle, one to the forest, one called Madho Singh, are there others?)

To catch some of the magic of the mountains, I dip into Frank Smythe's 1931 classic, *The Valley of Flowers,* where he wrote: 'I met a true civilization, for I found contentment and happiness. I saw a life that is not enslaved by the time factor; that is not obsessed by the idea that happiness is dependent on money and materials.'

Nowhere is this truer than at Gulabrai, Rudraprayag, where Jim Corbett shot on 1 May 1926 a man-eating leopard that had killed 125 people. Years later, he chanced upon a soldier crippled in the Great War, who had been a little boy on that celebrated day of years ago. He wrote:

> A typical son of Garhwal, of that simple and hardy hill-folk; and of that greater India, whose sons only those few who live among them are privileged to know. It is these big-hearted sons of the soil, no matter what their caste or creed, who will one day weld the contending factions into a composite whole, and make of India a great nation.

Slowly, percolating almost one at a time, I learnt about the innumerable legends of the Himalaya. In other places, I found the mountain folk in those deep valleys between dark forests and glistening scarps of snow, living with little else than the other gods—gods of the ice and the storm. In remote valleys they still depend upon the imps and the goblins, whom only witchcraft can appease. Around simmering campfires, I listened to tales of their malevolence and the ways by which it might be diverted.

From the ruins of the old forts, with the wind shredding the mist, I looked away from the crumbling walls, where above me rose the orchards, white with their blossoms as the snows of the Himalaya high above them or the foam of the river at their feet.

Far and wide now, the land extended on every side of me, orchards and fields and foaming rivers flanked by the hillside, black with deodars and over-topped by the snow-encumbered hills.

Sitting under the shade of a huge rock, snatches of Lama Govinda spring to my mind: 'Pilgrims are religious nomads, people who go with a purpose, think as they go, move for a reason. They have constancy in flux, patterns in variety, knowledge of the void.'

I believe that going to the Himalaya or even living there for a short time furthers one's development more than visiting holy men. But most folks cannot stay in these mountains for too long. The energy is too pure, too intense.

Poets tell us that there are treasures buried deep within the mountains and I too had set out to look for them. Only to discover that what we really crave lies buried within. We only have to look into the recesses of our cranium.

On one such trip, as I descended, soaking wet in summer's downpour, I was not amused

Winter spreads its ample mantle of snow and ice in the hills

till a fellow trekker going in the opposite direction winked at me and said: 'Don't let the drizzle get you down.' With a twinkle in his eye he added: 'Just think what it does for the rhododendrons!'

The battle cry of the movement for a separate hill state still resonates in my ears. Perhaps, in retrospect, you could say it was well and truly a people's clarion call of anguish at years of consistent neglect. Enough was enough and to the last man standing we had all taken the plunge.

Sadly, precious agonising years have been wasted in preparing a ground map for the future. We have yet to realise our full potential to ensure that we reverse the exodus. Men like my father must no longer stand at bus stops looking for the cheapest fare to get away from here. The day when young folks begin to stay on, progress would have arrived in these abandoned villages.

Uttarakhand is the custodian of pilgrimage destinations in ecologically fragile zones, and the ham-handedness of our planners is the last thing we need. We should simply leave the rest alone.

What do we need? You may fondly ask. The answer is a will to provide: water to the villages; teachers in the schools; proper health facilities; structures in harmony with our surroundings; clean public facilities; proper sewage control; regular electricity and employment for the young.

Enough damage has been done.

And in the ultimate analysis, Nature always triumphs over the puny machinations of men.

Ganesh Saili

Himalayan
Magic

Beyond the treeline lie the eternal snows. With global warming, the glaciers are now retreating

From underneath the earth you soar above; O Himalaya, the loftiness of your peaks and your mind are alike.

— Kalidasa

To the ancient poets of Uttarakhand, the land north of Haridwar is known as 'Paradise Ground' and apart from this land, what remained, other places, was called the Earth.

Little wonder then that the Himalaya has always been a source of attraction. We've conquered some of its mighty peaks. But are those peaks ever vanquished? Or have men panted and struggled to the top for a short-lived victory?

To those of us who live in these mountains, to those who call it home, this is the way it should be. To us, these peaks are a wilderness apart, not just a place for men, but the abode of the gods where these regal monoliths echo a sense of the eternal. 'We never grow tired of each other, the mountain and I,' said the Chinese poet Li Tao Po.

And mountain magic—there's something in it, that once having brushed you, never can you be the same again. Its sparkle never diminishes as it sweeps across the brow of India in a swathe for some 1,500 miles from east to west, between the Indus and Brahmaputra rivers with a width of just a hundred miles, forming a four-mile high physical barrier between the dusty, hot plains of India to the south and the windswept upland plateau of Tibet to the north.

Down the ages, they continue to defy the written word. Men have vainly tried to

Moraines of Gangotri after the glaciers have receded

describe the ethereal beauty, its overwhelming immensity, the primitive majesty and splendour, but have been unable to match Nature's grandiose works of architectural wonder.

To mountain folk, they are not just another range; they are an inseparable part of Indian consciousness, representing eternal values. Their grandeur makes us aware how puny we really are, for there is no scale against which one can measure them. They are not a single wall of ice-draped mountains, sprung from the womb of geological forces. But down the centuries, they have been contorted, twisted, and modified by erosion into a complex pattern. Numerous rivers have scoured great gorges across the ranges, whilst every year, the monsoons have continued to batter their southern aspect.

Top: Roopkund

Bottom: Ganga descends from the satin-finished rocks at Gaurikund

To understand this complex web of mountains, we can divide them into three zones. Imagine three crumpled folds of the earth's crust shoved upwards by gigantic forces. Begin at the northernmost edge of the vast plains, you would find the low hills of the Siwaliks, almost up to the foothills, where the Terai is populated by a variety of wildlife: tigers, elephants, and bears. In this fairy-tale forest, any moment Snow White and her seven dwarfs may steal out, only to rush back again once they spot mere mortals lurking around. Beyond the low-lying hills, rises the Lesser Himalaya with peaks averaging around fifteen thousand feet. Above these tower the Great Himalaya, twenty thousand feet is ordinary here. There are over a thousand such peaks. And beyond, stretches the immensity of the Tibetan Plateau.

Gangotri Temple built by Amar Singh Thapa and later renovated by the Maharaja of Jaipur

Wise men of the East, sages, poets, mendicants, and mystics have found themselves wandering to the northern ramparts of India. And they continue to do so. You wonder why they go to the snow-clad peaks, remote valleys and lost gorges, and mystical rivers looking for peace and solitude. Up here, more aloof from the bustle of life than anywhere else on earth, the raised snows proffer a pledge of peace, a promise of everlasting repose, of being whole again. For centuries, men from the plains of India have looked northwards at these summits culminating in shining whiteness. It is here, they believe, that the gods dwell. The intrepid ones moved towards them, penetrating their inner depths, looking for answers from the powers that ruled human destiny. In normal circumstances, they would ascend a river to its source, in a quest for spiritual powers. As Sir Francis Younghusband puts it:

© TS Chauhan

Numberless glacial-melt lakes like this fill up the mountains

> And to this day men from the plains of India come in hundreds to the Himalaya on the self-same quest—on the quest especially of that one Supreme Spirit whom men all over the earth have come to think must control all minor spirits and rule the world—and rule her for good ...

Get up close, breathe the sharp air and sense the monstrous presumption, and feel your spirit soar imperiously to dwarf all else. Wander awhile in the mysterious haze that envelops these mountains and be purified. Come and feel the power of this ultimate frontier at its grandest—the mightiest peaks, the most fearful precipices and the most terrific gorges and the largest glaciers. You may measure the peaks, or climb them, but they will reveal the ultimate challenge of our age—for the more you have seen, the more you have missed. As a Tibetan proverb puts it, 'There's only one escape from the crowds—live in the sky among the clouds.'

The Himalaya is at the very centre of the cosmology of the Hindus. The peaks are but the unfolding petals of the Golden Lotus that the God Vishnu created as a stepping stone on the path to the creation of the Universe. Mount Kailash is the solitary dwelling of Shiva where He sits in perpetual meditation, generating the spiritual force that sustains our cosmos. The mountain remains a lodestone to the followers of many faiths.

We are told: 'In the midst of such peaks one can draw near to what is truly placeless, the really divine.' We've been told that men climb mountains

Thalesagar peak at 6,904m looms large over Kedar Tal at 5,000m

© TS Chauhan

'Because they are there!' But do men really conquer those angry fangs snarling at the sky?

The debate rages on.

'What is the secret of it?' asks Francis Younghusband again: 'Quite certainly it is the power of the mountains to force the best out of men. Man likes to be his best. But often nothing short of a Himalayan peak can extract it from him—can compel him to be the fittest in body, alertest in mind and firmest in soul.' 'By climbing mountains,' wrote Wilfred Noyce, 'by extending himself beyond the bounds of everyday experience, a man can set up a new relationship with something bigger than himself.'

To the simple-minded, climbing a peak is the 'conquering' of a colossus. But nothing could be further from the truth. In 1936, to Bill Tillman, it was sacrilege, as he came down from Nanda Devi: 'The feeling which predominated over all was one of remorse at the fall of a giant.'

Frank Smythe, who discovered the Valley of Flowers in 1931, wrote of his ascent:

> It was as though I had been led blindfold up the mountain, and the bandage had been removed on the summit. But of all my memories, one stands pre-eminent: the silence. The silence of dead places where not even a plant grows or a bird dwells ... I seemed on the very boundary of things knowable and unknowable.

Two years later, he found himself crossing the pale of the unknown en route to Everest, as he felt convinced that he was roped to another phantom climber. So crystal clear was this feeling that he divided his piece of cake into two. The illusion

Garhwal Himalaya as seen from Masrana village

continued as he climbed. Then he saw two kites suspended motionless in the air.

Reinhold Messner, the 'King of Climbers' or the 'Magician', as he was called, once said: 'I don't feel alone. I instead sense a companion. There's always that someone to keep me company when I reach these altitudes on my own. Perhaps it's that partner within me.'

As Major Narendra Dhar Jayal, better known as Nandu Jayal who died at Camp V (21,000 feet) on Cho Oyu, said to his friend John Dias: 'John D., in all this beauty I guess God must be pretty close.' He died like he lived—he just couldn't care less:

> I've lived a life of travel and adventure. I have had the best, and, I go with no regrets. I am dying in the mountains I love. See that my bearer is looked after and that all I have goes to my sister, Mrs. Mitra. Just bury me around here some place.

The paradox of these mountains holds one in thrall: who really climbed Everest first? Could the gallant deaths of George Leigh Mallory and Andrew Irvine in 1924 cast a veil over the truth? Did they reach the top? And did they die descending or was it the other way around? There are no answers.

What we do know is that the ascetics of the East, in times gone by, were looking for more than just subduing a peak. Could it be that in these icy places man could finally be alone with his gods? Dr Paul Brunton in the 1930s wrote:

> Why do I love these mountains? Is it not partly because they tangibly reflect something of that stillness, that beauty which I find in my intangible meditations?

Thus it is that to look out of my window each morning becomes for me a veritable act of worship. With each glance I give my homage to Himalaya and enter into a mood of reverent adoration. These mountains stand in symbolic relation to our race. These snow covered colossi, like stupendous pointing fingers, indicate for me the lofty aspiration which must ever keep man from sinking into the grovelling existence of the gutter, whilst their unsullied whiteness beckons him to a purity which he has yet to attain.

Only those who have dwelt a while with such a horizon, filled with an array of shimmering white snow peaks, jutting clear-cut against the sky, can appreciate the intoxication that comes with early morning as one gazes upon it.

Ghagharia—the last halting place before the Valley of Flowers

And there is many a tale of heroism. To save the life of a Japanese climbing Mt. Kun, D. K. Sharma, liaison officer, set off after midnight, alone on an inhospitable night. It held the glacier in a vice-like grip. The sky was all ink with thick clouds. It was snowing with strong winds blowing. He plunged into the dark to get to Kargil. As he was looking for a track or some familiar sign on the glacier, his eyes were arrested by something moving in the direction of the Morino glacier. He had porters' tales of dead climbers walking in the night. Fear swelled inside him, giving him gooseflesh. He stood frozen while the shadows kept moving. What could it be? Very soon the mystery was solved: two bears, mother and baby were foraging for food. He moved on with the bears barely a few metres away, pretending he hadn't seen them, and was able to shake off the pursuing bears ... after a long tedious struggle, he was able to reach the road head and find help.

Of the rare creatures in these high mountains, the one that has grabbed the human imagination is the Abominable Snowman or the Yeti. We find Frank Smythe seeing some tracks in the snow,

which he took to be those of a man, though there were no shepherds around. On closer inspection it turned out to be the imprint of a huge naked foot, apparently a biped, and its strides closely resembling a man's tracks. What was it? wondered Smythe, as he set about photographing it.

'Bad *Manshi!'* said Wangdi, and then '*Mirka!*' And in case he still did not understand, '*Kang Admi* (Snowman).' Smythe observed:

> On the level the footmarks were as much as 13 inches in length and 6 inches in breadth, but uphill they averaged only 8 inches in length, though the breadth was the same ... There were the well-defined imprints of five toes ... Lastly there was what at first sight what appeared to be the impression of a heel, with two curious toe-like impressions on either side ...

Land of the Gods beckons the faithful from times immemorial

The agile creature had gone down the mountain like an expert climber, zigzagging down a series of ridges and gullies. His track down the glacier was masterly; he had cunningly avoided concealed crevasses.

'Obviously,' mused Smythe, 'the "Snowman" was well qualified for membership of the Himalayan Club.'

But you don't have to be a member of any club to see the stars through the thin, keen atmosphere of the high Himalaya. It is a memory that shall stay with you: the sky crowded with innumerable archipelagos of brilliant fire, so near that a hand outstretched could tear it down from heaven. Beneath these serene eyes the mountaineer must forget his little woes.

A fairy temple or Pari Mandir in the hills near Chakrata

Elsewhere the enigma of these mountains continue to weave a spell all of its own. We have Jim Corbett, the legendary shikari-turned-conservationist, who tracked and hunted down man-eaters. He once found himself arriving at dusk with a local government official, and the *tehsildar* insisted on risking a walk in the dark to a village, several miles away, rather than just spending the night in the dak bungalow. No one knows what exactly transpired with the great hunter who stayed alone or at least tried to. He would never talk about it. What we do have is a letter from a friend explaining why the *tehsildar* was so keen to put lots of distance between him and that bungalow.

> Jim and a friend arrived at a very isolated Dak bungalow late one evening and prepared to stay the night. However, after getting a scratch meal, neither of their bearers would remain at the bungalow and went off for the night.
>
> Jim and his friend occupied separate rooms and Jim had a hurricane lamp on a table beside his bed. He was extremely weary after a long day hunting a man-eater, but about 1 am he woke up suddenly to 'feel' as he put it an indescribable evil presence in the room. His light was then extinguished and he found his friend already there having suffered a similar experience, and he assured me that nothing would ever induce him to stay at the bungalow again!

These encounters with the supernatural were to become a part of his life. In September 1938, thirty-one years after he bagged the Champawat tigress, he was out tracking down the Thak man-eater. Sitting atop his *machan,* he heard an ear-splitting scream—an 'Ar-Ar-Arr' fading away into a long note—from a deserted village. As he put it:

> The scream had been the despairing cry of a human being in mortal agony, and reason questioned how

© TS Chauhan

Left: At 6,904m, Thalesagar peak looms over the 5,000m Kedar Tal in the Gangotri region

Right: Tourism supports the economy on which depend 20 lakh people

such a sound could come from a deserted village. It was not a thing of my imagination, for the dog had heard it and had abruptly stopped barking, and the sambhar had dashed away closely followed by her young one ...

Earlier, in 1929 he found himself at the holy hill of Purnagiri above a gorge on the Sarda River. It had been a gruelling trek of sixteen miles on a hot day through the sweltering Terai. As he sat back smoking an after-dinner cigarette, three lights appeared on the hill on the far side of the river. Presuming them to be the burning of deadwood in Nepal, he was forced to change his view as more lights appeared. Maybe it was some rich zamindar that had sent out a search party to look for some valuable he'd lost, he mused.

At daybreak, there was no sign of human habitation or of burning either. He wrote: 'Where the lights had appeared was perpendicular rock where no human being, unless suspended from above, could possibly have gone.'

Purnagiri, dedicated to the Goddess Bhagbatti, the goddess of plenty, is visited by thousands of pilgrims each year. The climb to the highest shrine is for those favoured by the gods while the lower one is open to all.

These moving lights are visible only to the especially favoured, and Corbett muses: 'This favour was accorded to me and to the men with me, because I was on a mission to the hill folk over whom the goddess watches ... '

And soon after, he put an end to the marauding Talla Des man-eating tigress. In eight years of its fearsome reign, it had killed 150 people.

The mountain goddess Nanda Devi keeps a watchful eye over her worshippers in Garhwal and Kumaon. The successful exploration of the Garhwal-Kumaon Himalaya began in 1934 with the arrival of Eric Shipton and H.D. Tilman.

But our story begins with these two coffee growers in Kenya, living on farms 160 miles apart.

On Eric's plantation was a 200-foot-high tooth of granite, an inconvenience on a farm, but a blessing to those who loved climbing. They began their first climb on this jutting rock face on the face of Africa thereby laying the foundation for one of the most famous mountaineering relationships.

The sedge is withered from the lake and no flowers bloom!

In January 1934, they decided on a combined attempt at the forcing of the Rishi gorge and the Nanda Devi basin. Eric's desire for simplicity and economy found a devout follower in Tilman which resulted in a trip of five months in the company of three Sherpas in the Himalaya, at a cost of just 140 pounds, including fares out and back to England in a cargo vessel!

They set out to discover a route into the inner basin at the foot of Nanda Devi, the 'inner sanctuary', to make a fairly accurate map of it and to find out if the mountains could be climbed by a larger party.

Since 1883, no less than nine attempts had been made to penetrate the basin or to set foot on

'the pearl of the Central Himalayas'. Of these early attempts, Hugh Ruttledge wrote:

> Nanda Devi imposes upon her votaries an admission test as yet beyond their skill and endurance: a 70-mile barrier-ring on which stand twelve measured peaks over 21,000 feet high, and which has no depression lower than 17,000 feet, except in the west where the Rishi Ganga, rising at the foot of Nanda Devi and draining an area of some 250 square mile of ice and snow, has carved for itself what must be one of the most terrific gorges in the world. Two internal ridges, converging from the north and south upon this river, form as it were the curtains of an inner sanctuary, within which the great mountains soars up to 25,660 feet.

Hugh Ruttledge's place is at the forefront amongst those early commissioners of Kumaon who had a feel for the place. Following in the footsteps are able administrators like Traill and Atkinson.

The *Himalayan Gazetteer* of 1888 makes special mention of the remoteness of the place:

> It appears like a spire of graying rock sprinkled with snow and lying to the north-east of Trishul and north-west of Nanda Kot and rising far above the similarly snow-clad summits which surround it. The summit is altogether inaccessible. The natives maintain that smoke is sometimes seen to issue from its summit, which they regard as the kitchen of the local deity.

To the locals, Nanda Devi is the benevolent mountain goddess, a mother who can grant boons or destroy those who stray from the chosen path. The legend of Nanda Devi has it that the daughter of a Garhwal chieftain escaped to the mountains and took refuge there. You will find her temples in Almora and other places in Garhwal. In the hills, you will hear stories of Traill, the first commissioner, who was struck blind because, disturbed by the festivities of the pilgrims, he had moved the Nanda Devi temple from near his office in the Badhan Fort to Almora, and that he regained his sight only when he begged her for forgiveness. Atkinson gives us another version of the tale:

Anjani Sain in Tehri Garhwal where schools like this bring education to the hills

> When the British took possession of Kumaon, the revenue-free villages attached

to the temple were sequestrated by Mr. Traill. In 1818, he was on a visit to the Bhotiya valley of Juhar, and whilst passing by Nanda Kot, where Nanda Devi is supposed to hold court, was struck blind by the dazzling colour of the snow. The people all told him that unless the worship of the goddess was restored, his temporary snow-blindness would remain forever, and on promising to this effect, his eyes were opened and healed.

Perhaps Kipling caught this elusive magic of these mighty mountains as he exhorted explorers:

... Go and find it.
Go and look behind the Ranges—
Something lost behind the Ranges.
Lost and waiting for you. Go!

Come to the mountains. Find out what it is to be a believer. It is not only poets who can feel their magic. Who knows what awaits you? Feel that eerie tingle; discover that the shadows fall not upon you alone:

Who is the third who walks always beside you?
When I count, there are only you and I together
But when I look ahead up the white road
There is always another one walking beside you
Gliding wrapt in a brown mantle, hooded
I do not know whether a man or woman
But who is that on the other side of you.'

—T. S. Eliot

Glorious Garhwal

The little village of Kharsali is the winter abode of the priests of Yamnotri

If you think of Garhwal, you see a small stream, a tributary of the Yamuna or the Ganga, rushing along the bottom of a steep rocky valley. On the banks of the stream and on the terraced hills above, there are small fields in which are grown maize, potatoes, spinach, rice and barley, and sometimes apples, apricots and peaches. Above the village are forests of pine and deodar, oak and rhododendron. But not every hillside is covered with foliage. Many are rugged and bare; some are masses of quartz and granite. On slopes most exposed to the wind, only grass and small shrubs can possibly hope to obtain a foothold.

Such a landscape is typical of Garhwal, with the districts of Chamoli, Pauri, Tehri, Uttarkashi and Dehradun forming one of India's northerly regions, whose massive snow ranges border Tibet. For a continuous distance of 200 miles the peaks constantly reach a height of 22,000 to 25,000 feet above sea level. Arrayed to the east, cloaked in mist and morning clouds, are the snow massifs of the mountain kingdom of Nepal.

I had grown up on a magic roll call of the mighty glaciers of Uttarakhand: Pindari, Milam, Sundar Dhunga (behind Nanda Devi), Gangotri, Chetrangi, Khatling, Jumdar, Bamak and Dukhroni. A glacier moves flowing down from high mountain peaks through rocky valleys, carrying off snow compacted over ages into a solid creeping mass serenaded by a madrigal of creaks and percussive cracks, a reminder that you are lying on a moving river of ice. It was there, every summer, into the very heart of lake and glacier country in north central Uttarakhand, that I once went to. It was there camping and freezing, exploring and discovering lost paths that I came to love it in the special way one loves a child.

And so if you were to tell me that a lake is just a body of water, I would take you by the hand to the sparkling waters of numberless *tals* or lakes: Sahastratal, Duirital, Dodital, Kadaktal, Vasukhital, Masartal, Kakbushandital, Sattal, Nainital, Bhimtal, Bhadarsartal and Nachketatal.

And it is not upon you alone that the spell works its charm. Lionel Terray, an early traveller, wrote: 'I hurried still more not to miss the vision for which we had come so far. Then the miracle happened. Folded in light mist, hill after hill rolled away into the distances from beneath my feet, and over this green ocean sparkled the vast icebergs of the Himalaya.'

Shrouded in the mists of antiquity are the many legends of the birth of the Ganga. Once upon a time there lived a king named Bhagirath, whose ancestors were reduced to ashes by a curse. The devout king

Badrinath Temple on the banks of the Alaknanda River

Facing page: A bend in the Ganga

Nauti village's festive air at the time of the Raj Jaat Yatra

did penance to bring the Goddess Ganga down from the heavens. But the goddess was apprehensive of her torrential fall from the heavens which could destroy the Earth. However, the prayers of King Bhagirath caused Ganga to fall from Heaven to Earth, while Shiva caught her midway in his matted locks, thus mellowing down the force of the fall of the river and averting Earth's destruction.

The king then mounted his chariot and rode ahead of the waters to the spot where the ashes of his ancestors lay. With him came a procession of gods, nymphs, demons, ogres and sages. Wherever the chariot went, the river followed meekly in its wheel ruts and all of Creation bathed in the holy waters that washed away all sins.

Venerated by Hindus, the river of faith holds one in thrall. Millions believe that to bathe in her waters is to be cleansed from sin, and at death ask no more but that their ashes be cast upon its waters.

According to one legend, the morning and evening *aartis* were performed at Badrinath and Gangotri by the same priest. This implies that the priest covered a distance of five days in a single day. How was it done? No one knows. The enigma remains.

And, along the route to Gaumukh is the ancient town of Barahat now known as Uttarkashi. Centuries ago, the Chinese traveller Hiuen Tsang passed through here on his travels recording his observations: 'They produce gold and for ages a woman has been the ruler and so it is called the kingdom of a woman. The husband of the reigning woman is called "king", but he knows

The icy secrets of Roopkund. Carbon dating and DNA tests of skletons reveal pilgrims from Kanauj who perished in a freak storm

nothing of the affairs of the state. He manages the wars and sows the land.'

Off the Alaknanda valley lies the mysterious lake of Roopkund below the shadow of Trishul. Briefly, in summer, the lake thaws to reveal the skeletons of travellers who perished there aeons ago. King Yashdhawal's regal pilgrimage met their icy fate in avalanche and storm 600 years ago. For them, there was no escape. Follow in their footsteps and you will be hard put to find a place to pitch a tent beyond Kelua Vinayak. The raindrops at your feet turn to ice on frozen stone. This is the 'Ocean of Rocks'—Shailsagar. Up a couple of zigzags and you are at Roopkund. Along the edge are the skeletal remains of that fateful Raj Jaat Yatra. But the clouds triumph once again. One snowflake meets another and a waltz begins.

And if you'd like to get away for a while, there's always Duirital, a lake set like an emerald in the heart of the inner Himalaya, reflecting one of the most stupendous panoramas in Garhwal, the Chaukhamba massif arrayed on the northern edge with mountains piled on mountains.

Even though there shall be a murmuring of water at your feet, the silence will seem complete.

They say that nature always reserves her treasures for those who walk quietly. Arrive here in the dead of winter, when this mountain wilderness is enjoying its rest from visitors, the forests teeming with many kinds of mammals, birds, plants is an extraordinary record—like a great open book—reaching back millions of years. And each step takes us to the shadowy beginnings of life. •

Trekking the Garhwals

A lone trekker heading towards his destination irrespective of the trecherous road ahead

Innumerable times, a question has been flung at me. 'Can you suggest a simple trek? The kind of place one can get to without loads of equipment, rock climbing or crossing glaciers and maybe getting lost?'

I know the feeling. Many of us would like to get a feel of the high mountains while not losing our way in a maze of icy waste.

Luckily there *is* such a place! Pack your bags anytime between April and October to surrender yourself to the central Himalaya. The first few days shall go by in an ambrosial blur. The trail shall take you through glades of juniper and dwarf birches, blue pine and rhododendron, and thundering waterfalls, enchanted boulder gardens, bubbling streams. Lost amidst a host of oak and maple, rhododendron and deodar are the enchanted waters of Dodital. Just two days away from the madding crowd and you will get 'the smell of the Himalaya—composed of rotting pine cones, damp wood smoke and dripping undergrowth,' as Kipling called it. Just some 400 km from Delhi and a comfortable twenty-one kilometre walk and you will reach your destination.

On a clear autumnal day, all you'll hear is birdsong if not the thumping of your own heart. Tumbling through the mossy-floored forests are the many sounds of silence, broken, if at all, by the chatter of black Himalayan pheasants or the doleful song of the green barbet. The ten-acre lake holds a population of brown trout, which in the 1890s, the Maharaja of Tehri asked a far-sighted Englishman to help stock. Happily, because of his efforts, Dodital has a unique population of brown and Himalayan rainbow trout.

At 3,750m, a trekker on the highest peak in the Himalayas poses in a hat and shorts

In the rugged mountains one finds chequered a few lonesome dwellings. Most of the population live in the Terai and lower hilly regions. Although it is a thinly populated area, it could not possibly sustain any more people than it does now. Invariably, Garhwali cultivators are poor, some very poor, but they are sturdy and have wonderful powers of endurance, and they manage to wrest a precarious living from the unhelpful soil.

Or take a typical hill village, its rough stone-houses straddling the spur of a hill, above terraced fields, above the stream or river. Off the beaten track, it attracts few outsiders. There are usually a half-dozen families belonging to the village, each having a few acres of land on which everyone works, cultivating the rugged terrain, isolated by mountains, at the mercy of the weather gods. Women are the backbone of the homestead. In the small fields, they join in sowing, weeding and reaping. Their labour never ceases as day after day, a bit at a time, they subdue the precipitous slopes to cultivation. Sometimes, women are the only ones working on the fields. This is not because the men have run away. It means that the land cannot provide enough food. In the continuing male exodus from the hills, the men have had to take jobs in the plains to keep the hearth fire burning back at home. Sadly this turns villages into refugee camps inhabited only by women and children, by grannies and aged men. Ironically, women who spend most of their day in ever-increasing search for fodder, fuel and water have been at the forefront of environmental movements like Chipko (hugging the trees) and the Uttarakhand movement for a separate hill state.

It's no easy task making a living from the calcinated soil up in the hills

From an early age, children help in the fields, grazing cattle or carrying milk to the market. Yet the hunger for learning is ever-present, and one will find children walking five or six miles to school every day.

In the riverine valleys of Garhwal, the food is simple: milk, lentils, a few vegetables, a little fruit and, sometimes sheep or goat—shikar, they call it! Walking along the streams, you could probably spot a boy, all of ten years old, trapping fish 'Garhwali-style'—a wicker-trap called a *jibala* is placed along the narrow part of the waters; a pulpy paste of *timru* bark is thrown into the stream; the natural astringent stuns the fish and in the trap, a pandemonium of fish lies quivering.

But no such anaesthetics await you and me, or the much-touted 'common man'. Medical facilities are hard to come by, where you will usually find an ill-equipped dispensary with a compounder in charge. Invariably, the doctor will be on leave. The sick, either women or children, often have to walk great distances to reach a hospital. At times the ailing simply stay at home until they get better—or fail to get better.

Many roads are either mule-tracks or footpaths and, although new roads have opened several remote areas, large tracts of Garhwal cannot be reached except on foot. As you bounce along some of these eyeball-rattling dirt roads, remember that a letter from a Garhwali living in, say, Mussoorie may take one to three weeks to reach his village in Chamoli, though as the crow flies the distance is no more than a hundred miles.

Some villages have primary or middle schools, but to send a child to college, which entails sending them to live in a town in the foothills, involves great expense and hardship for the parents. Of course the Garhwal University is now headquartered in Srinagar. Colleges affiliated to this university are scattered throughout the region. But the major concentration is in the towns. Educational facilities are still scarce in the hills, because those who are fortunate enough to receive a good education generally do rather well. There are many Garhwali scholars, educationists and professionals of note.

Temporary *chaans* are hutments of wandering shepherds grazing sheep in the meadows

True, some 'progress' has come to these mountains too. When it comes to a potential catastrophe, we cannot sell Mother Nature short; to us, an example of this is in the hot, dusty town of Tehri, now submerged by the waters of a great dam.

It is not here alone that the dark patches fall. The 'dark' leaves its imprints all over these mountains. Going through the area, you will spot a legion of such visible symbols of progress too! Electricity lines without power, pipelines without water, schools *sans* teachers, hospitals without beds, and dispensaries without medicine—a cobweb of inequity spread over the hills like fine muslin.

An old proverb in the hills has it: '*Aphyun maryan bina swarg ney dikhdoh*' meaning one cannot see heaven without first dying. This fact came home to roost some summers ago when the forests caught fire; while for some, it is easy to get caught up in the elitist euphoria that the reserved forests are 'special sanctuaries'.

This is untrue. They exist only by democratic decree. Once ablaze, the people were already alienated by the curtailing of their traditional rights and the fretting forest officials got no support from the people.

'If it is *their* forest—let them put out their *own* fires!' shrugged the hill folk.

Perhaps community forestry, under the watchful eye of women's groups, would be the obvious answer. But who is listening?

'We live here,' pleaded a local to us, 'while tourists think the Himalaya is only a backdrop and we're but characters in a play.'

Meanwhile, higher up in the mountains, the autumn wind carried with it a whiff of winter, where the streams are edged with a delicate filigree of ice crystals. Many climbers have been drawn by the glory of the ranges, beckoned, as it were, by the soaring summits that loom above as far as the eyes

Young trekkers taking a break to enjoy the view

can reach. The mountains, looming out of leaden thunderclouds, were driven inch by inch, five miles into the sky. The sweep of blossoming mustard fields, apricot groves and wild flowers ablaze at dawn is indelibly etched upon their psyche.

The Garhwalis have their pleasures too. Almost everyone can sing. Among musical instruments, they favour the *bansuri* (the shepherd's pipe) and the drum. As many have to earn their living far away from home, most songs deal with the pangs of separation from parents, loved ones or home in the hills. One song has it:

Oh, mountain swift, you are from my father's home—
Speak, Oh speak in the courtyard of my parents,
My mother will hear you:
She will send my brother to fetch me,
A grain of rice alone in the cooking pot,
Cries: 'I wish I could get out!'
And I wonder—
Will I ever reach my father's house?'

Many legends are associated with birds. There is a legend here that the wedge-tailed green pigeon is the reincarnation of a moneylender, who died of grief at the unfair end of a lawsuit. In a mild long whistle, his plaint rises to the heavens: '*Un-nee-ow! Un-nee-ow!*' which means 'Injustice! Injustice!'

Another fine singer is the sunbird. But perhaps the finest songster is the grey-winged ouzel. Throughout the early summer he makes the hillsides resonate with his

Humans are but ants before the grand and majestic mountains

'How can he make mistakes?' exclaimed Shahji, furrowing his brow, 'the fool does *no* work!'

There was little I could say. A strange figure on an amulet had caught my attention—a talisman to ward off the evil eye. It seemed to stare at me. I stared back. And I was hooked.

What began as a lark, a plaything of the moment and a willow-the-wisp turned into a passion. It followed me in my meanderings through every little dent in the mountains. At sunset, the dull glint of burnished metal became a beacon, leading me to dingy shops, as to an oasis in the formidable desert landscape, at the end of a day's journey.

Rummaging through a hand-rubbed chest, the silversmith would come up a winner with a stringed coin necklace, someone's precious heirloom that had found its way to the bazaar.

Strangely enough, I never came across a coin pre-dating the Gurkha War ending in 1812. There are no answers. It is as if the turbulent rivers had swept away a dark period of history, burying all in one eloquent silence.

Dipping into my Hobson-Jobson, I know that the *sicca* was abolished as a coin in 1836 and a universal medium of exchange of British territory called the rupee was introduced. It weighed 180 grams, of which 165 grams was pure silver.

This silver was also brought down through narrow mountain trails from Tibet. In earlier times, it had been imported into the country from those surrounding it.

But again, in 1820, the influx of British silver rupees brought the practice to a grinding halt. Lawder of the Geological Survey of India could not conceal his glee, exclaiming: 'The Bhotiyas state that our coin is largely preferred by the inhabitants there, to the coinage of other countries. They ask for the *cheharadar rupaya* or face-printed money!' The Tibetans themselves had, for ages, been selling wool, sheep and salt to Nepal, and buying in exchange, rice and silver coins.

The old pilgrim shelters of the Kedar Valley were wiped out in the flood

But records tell us that in 1751, the Seventh Dalai Lama had shot off a missive to the Nepalese, regarding the debasing of the coins with copper.

Nothing came of it, and things remained in limbo till 1775, when Prithvi Narayan demanded that the former debased coins be devalued, as the new coins were of pure silver. Reluctantly, the Khasag agreed to a slight reduction in the value of the old coins. In the spring of 1788, as the snow began to thaw and summer was a promise in the air, the Gurkhas marched into Tibet. It took four long years before they were ousted in 1792.

In Garhwal, the silversmith will rarely buy the more costly new silver. It is much easier to buy it from the mountain folk at a lower price. Did it bother him, I once asked, this smelting down of precious family heirlooms?

'I simply assay the ornaments that come in,' he mused, 'recognising at times the work of my own ancestors, but people come in here, asking for newer designs, and then the agents from the plains take it all away.'

However, what they cannot take away are the memories of snow-capped mountains, where women have, for centuries, mocked the thunder and laughed at the rain. It is in these remote places that silver will always remain the poor man's gold.

Of course, for those who seek a little more there are the village fairs. These can be a truly wonderful experience. Perhaps these should not be solely aimed at the outsider. The village folk can never be made secondary to external interests. They are not props in a play. It is time to take a call on whether we want a mela. It cannot and must not be reduced to a circus.

Lower down, in the villages, the short, stocky cows, typical of Garhwal, are perched on precipitous slopes that would alarm even a goat. Of course, well-intentioned attempts have been made to improve the stock—but the offspring cannot survive in the hills!

And no less demanding is the cultivation of the rugged terrain, isolated by the mountains, at the mercy of the gods; the Garhwalis are God-fearing. Sumer Singh Negi, seventy years old, says: 'We are the ants of Time,' and adds: 'Day by day, a little at a time, we have subdued these slopes for cultivation.'

People at a tented colony en route to Gaumukh

'Your *jhola*-types come often!' says a wizened old man, dismissing outside interference. 'They arrive in a pair of jeans, a bag slung over their shoulder and a five-hundred-rupee note in their pocket. At the end of their visit they have changed neither!'

Like mountain folk elsewhere, in Garhwal too there is a strong predilection for the supernatural and, in their folklore, tales of ghosts and demons mingle with legends of kings and heroes. You will find buried in these tales the early history of the mountains. The scholarly Tara Dutt Gairola, in collaboration with the Englishman Right Reverend E. S. Oakley, included many of these tales in a volume called *Himalayan Folklore*, published in 1934. This included access to material collected by Pandit Ganga Dutt Upreti, who was Senior Assistant Commissioner of Garhwal at the turn of the nineteenth century.

Most legends converge on the times of Raja Ajai Pal, born 1254, who subdued several minor chieftains to consolidate his rule. Legend and history mingle to intertwine the reigns of ruling families where several minor kings were constantly at war with each other. Up to the year 1700, weapons were bows and arrows, daggers and swords, occasionally bamboo staves while stones too were used to stunning effect.

The main Rajput families in these Himalayan districts were the Pals of Garhwal, the Chands of Champawat and the Katyur princes, who originally lived in Joshimath before migrating to the Katyur Valley in Almora.

Rajas followed each other to the throne of Garhwal, but it often happened that the real masters were the turbulent races on either side: the Rohillas, the Gujjars, the Sikhs and the Gurkhas—who levied heavy tithes upon the luckless cultivators. Later, in the closing years of the eighteenth century, the Gurkhas conquered Garhwal which indirectly led to the arrival of the British.

Capturing Almora in 1790, the Gurkhas carried out their invasion into Garhwal. Srinagar was taken in 1803, and Raja Praduman Shah escaped to the plains. Pawning his property and throne, he valiantly got an army together and returning to the foothills, attacked the invaders, but he was defeated and killed in Dehradun.

In the Gurkhas, the British found very stubborn opponents when they faced each other on Kalinga Hill in the Anglo-Nepalese war of 1814. The fierce men from Nepal had over-stretched their lines of communication and were eventually driven out of Garhwal. In 1815, Raja Sudershan Shah was given back the territory that lay west of the Alaknanda River, while the British retained the lands to the east—that is Pauri-Garhwal, which was called British Garhwal up until 1947.

Despite their military misfortunes, the Garhwalis were hardly poor fighters. But their isolation, small numbers and lack of proper weaponry made them easy prey for marauding armies. An organised defence was seldom possible.

The valour of Garhwali soldiers became known to the world when they fought in various European campaigns during World War I.

Others showed courage of another kind when Chander Singh Garhwali refused to open fire on unarmed protesters during the freedom movement. Their bravery has inspired generations of hill people.

Earthquake-hit Didsari village struggles to recover

Out of these mountains, 2,500 men walked thousands of miles to join the Azad Hind Fauj under Subhash Chandra Bose as it gathered in Singapore during World War II.

To the outsider, life in the hills may seem idyllic and the people simple. But for those who live here, life is far from simple, and is one long struggle. British travellers, botanists and mountaineers have gone into raptures over the simple living of the hill people, and we have Frank Smythe in *The Valley of Flowers*, writing:

> In Garhwal I met a true civilization, for I found contentment and happiness. I saw a life that is not enslaved by the time factor – that is not obsessed by the idea that happiness is dependent on money and materials. I had never before realised how much happiness there is in simple living and simple things.

Delectable words! If only you do not have to spend your entire life in some high-altitude village which is snowbound for four months in the year, with cultivation coming to a standstill in the weather-plagued fields. People have to manage with food gathered and stored during the summer months. The Garhwali will agree that there is happiness in simple things, but will qualify this by adding that he could be happier with some money and materials.

There are times when it is good to remind the visitor that Garhwal is no paradise. In geological terms, these mountains are, comparatively speaking, a recent happening. Grooved and ridged by the violent upheavals of its birth, with stupendous peaks of sheer rock rising above the treeline, or furious rivers with chasms as deep as sleep, or green vales next to barren slopes, it remains a land of sudden contrasts and awesome grandeur. Garhwal has never really ever been free from disputes, and has been commercially exploited, its hillsides quarried and its great forests clear felled.

A video-coach en route to Gangotri has broken down in the market place. Its blaring music blasts away. Chait Singh, who runs a provisions shop, watches me grimace. 'Their music is so unlike ours,' he ventures, adding: 'To me it mostly sounds like cats fighting.'

I guess it's the price these places pay as tribute to tourism—an unending cavalcade of vehicles spewing fumes as thick as smog in the diamond air; a tourist blight which spells the ruin of many a paradise. How many worms will make it into Eden in this apple? I wonder.

Presently, the video coach belches, starts with a pronounced stutter, grinds its way over the hill, and is soon lost in its own cloud of dust.

The sun comes out and a voice exclaims: 'See—I told you the monsoon is over!' With the warmth, the birds break out into song but the boom of the torrents ring through the gorge.

How much longer will these little out-of-the-way places retain their charm and music? Who knows?

Chait Singh simply says, 'Ha! It's all in the hands of the gods or the politicians! Will they ever learn to see beyond making money?'

I drive away, leaving him standing there, looking fresh and happy on the banks of the river. He has a point, I muse.

'The higher you stand, the further you see,' is an oft repeated saying in the Garhwal, especially for those who cling on to survival by a fraying thread.

Walking up the river, I see the distant slopes covered in white. There is something of the eternal in the Himalayan snow, or perhaps something as

On the edges of Roopkund

Facing page: In May 1889, at Mundali near Chakrata, a man-eating tiger was shot by B. B. Osmaston

close to the timeless as we may ever glimpse. What we do with this wilderness now will be read in the book of tomorrow.

'Look!' exclaims an old man, 'When the ferns begin to turn yellow, the seeds of the cobra-lily, red, and the walnut begins to shed its leaves, you can be sure the monsoon has ended.'

'Ha! Don't believe those old wives' tales. Look! It is still raining. The monsoon will end only when it stops raining!' says the impish fellow before scampering off into the downpour.

Higher up in the mountains, the August wind carries the scent of winter. Dark, ominous clouds rear their heads over the ranges, threatening snow.

The hills are hardly poor and unyielding. They have valuable timber, but the forests must be constantly renewed and replenished. They have valuable herbs. They have minerals. The Alkapuri Mountain near Badrinath, from where the river Alaknanda emerges, is reported to have gold deposits. The Dhunar community pans the lower stretches of the river, taking gold from the sands using ancient techniques. Copper deposits have been found by the Geological Survey of India in Dhanpur Patti of Ranigarh where a mountain is said to have rocks streaked with copper.

When these riches are carefully and fully exploited, when roads and communications are improved, when educational and medical facilities are expanded, only then will the people of the hills come, well and truly into their own.

Power, in the ultimate analysis, belongs to the people. ●

Not So Quiet Flows the Yamuna

Yamuna, the sister of Ganga, flows gently to parch the thirst of the plains

A howling wind rattles the windowpanes. Icy fingers rent the sky. Lightning falls on a distant tree and peals of thunder applaud this impassioned symphony of nature. A flash of lightning illuminates the bare mountains.

Somewhere, perhaps only in the mind, sounds a rhythmic pounding of drums. I get up, bathed in cold sweat.

Far, far away, I get a glimpse of the valleys of the Himalaya. I travel back in time to think of a sun-silvered stream spun into the Yamuna, gushing through chasms on a long journey to the plains of northern India. On the banks of the Yamuna, the dark sister of the Ganga, stands the quaint village of Lakhamandal.

Breaking the clods, an old man tills the rocky soil, as little grows in the north wind. His wooden plough turns the soil in the Biblical admonition: '... a time to plant, and a time to pluck up that which is planted; a time to kill, and time to heal; a time to break down, and a time to build up; ... '

Luckily, they were spared the attempts of do-gooders to change their way of life.

Of that early journey, memories survive: a rickety old bus rattling along a narrow trail winding up along the banks of the river. The road glistening wet, like a slithering snake in the autumnal drizzle. A nervous co-passenger asks the driver how he took the bus so fast around those hairpin bends.

'By shutting my eyes every time I'm scared!' explains the driver.

With those words for consolation, our eyes half-open, we shut our minds to the

The Pushpa Ganga in the Valley of Flowers

With the male exodus, sometimes our villages seem like sanctuaries for children, women and old men

hereafter which looms threateningly near.

Thatched roofs emit occasional streams of smoke from the teashops perched along the edge of the road. The mountains' huge masses of quartz and granite stand stark naked without a patch of green, their bleakness erupting into a dazzle of glory as the autumnal sun reveals itself in all its splendour.

The bus rattles to a halt at Kuan. The road dries up as the driver brings his foot down on a rusty footboard. The dampness evaporates and a cloud of dust rises in welcome, filtering through the broken glass-windows and settling on our clothes. In a minute, everyone appears to have aged a decade. Youth is, however, restored by slapping off the dusty coating that encrusted us.

Tired travellers, we straggle into a chai shop run by one Nain Singh, a tall, handsome youth from Lakhamandal. A wizened old man with a grey tobacco-stained moustache sucks noisily on his hookah. With a glint in his eyes, he says, 'Tomorrow is the Athward festival. You are just in time to witness the sacrifice of buffaloes to appease the angry gods.'

'Sacrifice? In this day and age?' I react.

He shrugs this off with a contemptuous 'Ha! Non-believers! What is the world coming to!'

'Why don't we use the ropeway bridge?' I ask Nain Singh, who offered to help us cross the river.'

'Too risky,' answers Nain Singh.

'Ritual sacrifice has nothing to do with the believing,' mutters the old crone.

Down below, the river gurgles at these futile disagreements.

The river had been there when the Pandavas spent a lonely exile along its banks. It was there when a young boy set off, to establish the four *maths*: Dwarka, Jagannath, Badrinath and Sringeri. The river had flowed, a silent spectator, down the course of legend—history.

The river is cold. Icy cold. Its waters, turbulent. A pack of mules is the first to wade across it. We brace ourselves for the crossing. The waters suddenly seem very deep and the rocks treacherously slippery. The mountains on the other side rise menacingly into the sky, their colourless hue adding a grim note to our silent train. I brave a look upwards. Immediately above, the hillside is lashed with caves. Legend has it that the Pandavas spent their exile wandering incognito in these wild mountains. At Lakhamandal, it is said, their scheming cousins, the Kauravas, built a palace of shellac in an abortive bid to get rid of their exiled cousins, the Pandavas.

A narrow path rises shrill as a scream piercing across the lower terraced fields. Apple, peach and apricot trees, now bereft of leaves, must colour the hillsides pink and white in spring. From a spur on a hillock, the rays of the setting sun wash the grey-tiled roofs of the distant houses with a reddening glow. Stretching out lazily before us is the land speckled with low-lying huts. The land of magic—Lakhamandal.

Snatches of tales told by my mother drift through my mind. Her voice whispers a familiar warning, 'Never go across the Yamuna, my son. Sometimes people get lost there.'

It only piqued my interest.

Around me, the whisper turns into a gentle pulsing. Rhythmic. Throbbing. As we near the village, it reverberates through a pounding of drums. Primitive. Sensual. The village suddenly looms large before

Timeless sacred rituals along the river are part of the heritage of the hills

Lakhamandal in the Yamnotri valley is rich in archeological finds

us. A temple rises above a cluster of houses. In the courtyard of the temple, a young boy beats a round drum slung from his shoulders. He smiles dreamily, lost in the fitful music that pounds through the valley.

'You play the drums well,' I say, mesmerised.

'You should have heard the one played last year,' he says caressing the taut skin, 'It was made of wolf-skin and its beat tore the drums made from lamb-skin.'

Knowing little about drums, I do not contradict him. After all, strange things happen in the mountains and then there is the indisputable fact that he knows much more about drums. More than I do.

We move towards the temple. Atop, a wooden canopy is perched rather precariously. Along the sides are littered exquisite sculptures dating from the eighth to sixteenth century. Two life-size statues of Mahabharata characters Arjun and Bheem stand propped up in the backyard, their faces mutilated probably during the Gurkha incursions at the end of the eighteenth century. My reverie is interrupted by a shrill cry of '*Chai, sahib*'. A glass of steaming tea is thrust at me. Some youngsters inspect our belongings with unabashed curiosity.

Refreshed, we adjust our backpacks and walk on towards Dhora—a stone's-throw from the temple at Lakhamandal.

'Must have been a *shivalingam* factory in the old days!' mutters my friend Misra as he surveys the stone wilderness that sprouts from the rocky earth. Truly an archaeologist's dream comes alive here.

The tired sun has set. Wisps of smoke begin to trail from the cooking-fires burning in the houses below.

Drums are an integral part of all celebrations in the hills

The mountain paths are obscured by the mist and lurking darkness. An apparition brings us to a sudden halt. Under a peepul tree, in front of a blazing bonfire, sits a picture-book sadhu. The glow from the fire bathes his classical lotus position in an unearthly light. He sits dragging at his *chillum,* surrounded by his disciples. His body covered with grit, grime and ashes from the holy fire. The darkness blanks out the stars and settles with the lingering mist over Lakhamandal to the fitful beating of drums.

I cannot sleep. Nor can my companions. Like me, their eyes await the slow lightening of the darkness in the east that will signal the break of dawn. Slowly, one by one, the stars are extinguished. Nature bestirs itself. A screeching flock of parrots alights on a wild fig tree; babblers scuttle the sparse

Tourists at Devprayag, all set for river rafting

bushes for breakfast. The noisy parrots burst away in a confusion of green as the drums beat their ritual rhythm. The sun crawls over the mountain tops, its rays pressing warmly against the cold earth. Smoke from the sadhu's subdued fire spiralling into an azure sky.

Lakhamandal awakens to a new day.

And so do we. Down at the stream, a rather young woman stops to stare at us as she fills her brass pitcher. A ray bounces a blinding gleam as she balances it on her head. Suddenly I know why my mother had never wanted me to come to this land. Who would want to return, once having caught a glimpse of such haunting beauty; who would want to leave these mountains?

The sun blazes in a clear sky. Clouds are bunched over snow-capped peaks near the horizon. The sadhu, his weathered skin hanging on him like ill-fitting clothes on a scarecrow, claims he has been fasting for eight days. By the look of him, he does not seem to have eaten after his shrill entry into this world. All he does is smoke his *chillum* and emit a guttural: '*Bholay Shanker*!'

On the surface, it all appears normal. But barely scratch the surface and you know that there is something in the air.

Gaily dressed crowds start streaming in at noon, like restless butterflies invading a placid pasture, from the nearby villages. Each procession of merrymakers is led by an imposing woman who walks up to the temple and plants her tribal flag in the crumbling walls of the temple. Yet the tension is there, you can reach out and grasp it. A pulsating energy emanates from the waiting crowd. The beat of drums reaches a wild crescendo as the headman of Lakhamandal makes a dramatic entry astride a white horse.

Tied with thick ropes, a buffalo is dragged into the open space by men armed with sticks. A blood-curdling cry gathers in the throats of all the idlers and shatters the peace as they begin to dance.

Is this the twentieth century? In answer to my doubt, an irate officer snaps: 'No photographs!' He has a certain mindlessness that is typical of a sense of power without reason. The cameras are slipped into their leathery tombs.

Meanwhile, the sadhu and the headman are arguing loudly. 'The gods must have their due. The sacrifice must be performed!' says the headman.

The sadhu is calm. With a raised hand he intones the consequences. 'All evil will come down on those who perform this slaughter,' he says in a clear voice. A hush falls over the gathering. As if in answer to the latter's prayers, a group of ragged boys pant up the hill. A crowd had by now gathered under the sprawling chestnut tree. The headman's horse lies dead.

A murmur runs through the crowd. All faces turn blankly towards the sadhu, who is already walking away in the distance. 'Must have been the sun,' exclaims the headman alluding to his horse, as two village urchins mutter the sadhu's departing curse that if the sacrifice is not stopped, the headman's eldest son will die within the week too. All eyes were fixed on the headman who had suddenly paled. But he recovers and gives a careless shrug. At a nod from him, the drums pick up their lost rhythm again. The ashes from the sadhu's holy fire are swept disdainfully away. A priest materialises out of nowhere and hurriedly anoints the doomed buffalo. The crowd surges forth excitedly, its fear, forgotten. After all, haven't the ancestors of the headman ruled the area with an iron fist? They should know better. What's there in a stupid sadhu? With one ceremonial blow, the buffalo's ear is sliced off.

Duirital above Ukhimath, is the perfect get away for those looking for solitude

Crazed with pain, it hunches, straining at its bonds. Sticks, swords, axes rain upon the enraged animal. A bugle peals as it breaks its bonds in one mighty lurch. But a frenzied mob crazily hacks it down. The crowd's savage appetite is sated.

Stunned, we turn our back on this bloody spectacle and walk down the mountain trail to the Yamuna. The sun sinks gravely behind the hills. We wash off the dust of Lakhamandal at the river, but not its memories. They return, to haunt us, on dark stormy nights. When the drums sound in the distance again. •

Travels with the Four-Horned Ram

A four-horned ram leads the Raj Jaat Yatra from Nauti village to Roopkund

It certainly was *not* his day. Shrieking like a monster the wind lashed the mountains white with its cat-o'-nine-tails. All day snow had been piling on the Trishul massif in the Garhwal Himalaya. Suddenly, with a resounding snap, it tipped. First a rumble, then a roar, growing louder into a wail—the echo of an avalanche. On cue, the shroud parted as the churning snow plunged towards them.

There was no escape. The twilight of eternity had begun in the narrow confines of Jyuar Gali or 'the path of death'. King Yashdhawal's pilgrimage led by a magical four-horned ram was doomed before it began. Through tortuous days, the priests of Nauti village had remonstrated but the King refused to budge. Throwing tradition to the winds, he insisted that the queen and the nautch girls must accompany him for Raj Jaat Yatra or the 'Royal Pilgrimage'.

Almost 600 years later, in the fall, we were to follow in his footsteps. On the very first day, accompanied by thunder and lightning, news trickled in of thirty-five people who had perished in a cloudburst barely two ranges away. Not the most auspicious of beginnings. Yet red in tooth and claw, nature has not always been kind to the gentle dwellers of the riverine valleys. Resigned to their fate, they say, '*Dev key maar nah khabar nah saar*'. How true! When the gods strike, there is neither logic nor reason.

This pilgrimage had occurred only four times in the last century: 1905, 1925, 1968 and 1987. For so arduous is the journey, so long and difficult—a three-week journey led by a four-horned ram during the peak of monsoon. The road-head ends at Barkhigadh, beyond which lie the temples of Kotkandhara, its entrance guarded by mute stone sentinels. In some fields above Dewal, crops grow in a perfect circle—a tradition dating back to the mists of antiquity. But why just a few bushels of wheat?

There are no answers—only enigma.

Ahead looms Loharjung—home to all pilgrims. The thirty odd families of the village fling open their doors to travellers. Today, a festive mood grips everyone as dance and song reverberate. The many-coloured headbands lend colour to the austere mountains.

Eighty-year-old Chattar Singh wraps a scarf around my head, adding: 'These colours signify different things: red for power, yellow for a bountiful harvest and blue for peace.'

And Loharjung lodges itself firmly in our hearts. No! Not the dance; or the arrows embedded in the trees (from wars in the past, you wonder); or a bell dangling from a limb; or the sprawling ranges—beyond all these is the earthy love of its people.

Perched atop a slate-roof at Wan village

Facing page: Ruins of the old Forestry College in Mundali

Everyone works on the land. Only Chattar Singh is exempt. On a bent cherry cane, he totters past our open window on his determined morning walk across the ridge.

Higher up, in lost wilderness, the clickety-clack of a gigantic clock beats in the shade—the heartbeat of watermills. The miller's boy plays truant from school. It is more fun tending to the flow of water. A delicate task, it is, with no margin for error. One mistake and the millstones shatter.

At Wan, the last village on the trail, live a hundred families. Above a slate-paved courtyard, the local grocer hoards his fair share of goods and gossip. Today he is in a garrulous frame of mind: 'Roopkund?'

'Yes! If we're lucky.'

'Look for the old postman; he has a stash of things he's found in the lake.'

'Treasures ... like what?'

'Beads, baubles and even a coin with an arrow drawn across it.'

'Where do I find him?'

'Around here if he's not on his rounds.'

We looked around for him. Still the postman proved elusive. Maybe he had decided to lie low with querulous strangers lurking around. Who knows?

Above Wan, lives a lone survivor of the Indian National Army, a warrior of the national movement surviving on tales of battles in lands forlorn. He's lost in a collection of dog-eared books. Sometimes, the last few pages are missing but that doesn't seem to bother him—he knows all the endings by rote. He also doubles as the village *bakya* or soothsayer. What do the stars hold for the day?

'The Chotta Raj Jaat won't reach here today!' he mutters ominously.

And sure enough it doesn't.

And, just to prove him right, a drunken squabble delays progress between Bankagaon and Loharjung.

At dusk we are witness to a poignant scene as groups of mountain folk, who had gathered to await the passing of the royal procession, return home heart-broken. In the inky darkness, their fiery stakes look like amber beads broken off from a necklace and scattered on black velvet.

Hidden close by in the sacred grove of Latu, lurks the mischievous herald of Nanda Devi, the hill goddess. If you go by the folksongs, she is forever making trouble. So wary are the hill folk of her depredations that the shrine, in an eerie setting—a stupendous deodar with each branch larger than a tree, festooned with moss and lichens—is rarely opened. Something in the atmosphere makes the blood creep, the nerves prick and tingle as Latu weaves an unseen spell.

Beyond this, the trail is reduced to one long slithery haul through slush churned up by buffaloes, cows and horses, the mud pulverised to microns. To take my mind off the immediate, I wander down memory lane, to my early days as I fumbled with Maths under the stern eye of Mr William Geyer, my teacher in school. Tugging at his goatee, he would pose a problem: 'A monkey climbs up a slippery pole, jumps three feet and slides back two. In how many jumps will he make it to the top of a thirty foot pole?'

Oh! I did try hard! But I could not work that one out. What has stayed with me though is the harried

A rare glimpse of the Goddess Nanda Devi at Wan village

look on the face of that poor monkey. Striding up this treacherous path, I know *this* monkey is not about to get too far.

Beyond the treeline are the ambrosial high-altitude meadows of Bedni and Aali Bugyal. Finally, they trudge, the priests and pilgrims, barefoot in single file, carrying parasols woven of birch bark fibres and stuffed with leaves. These are a unique symbol of Nanda Devi, considered pure, and are supposed to serve the twin tasks of keeping off the rain and sun as well as malevolent ghosts and demons. As they move, the goddess is supposed to move too.

At nightfall, ravenous clouds devour the sky, streaks of lightning turn the meadows into an amphitheatre of the gods, and peals of thunder mock the mountains. In a flapping tent, sleep comes fitfully. Drifting between reality and dreams, I see another king from another time: King Lear—a majestic old man draped in a flowing black robe, with a flowing beard, an escapee from an old painting, wandering the wind-swept heath in a storm, cursing the heavens.

Decorated four-horned ram heads the Raj Jaat Yatra

Watersheds of another kind are these meadows. They winnow the chaff from the grain, the men from the boys and so, at dawn, just a handful remains for the final assault.

Pather Nachauni or the Place of the Wicked Women is where Raja Yashdhawal's nautch girls were hurled to their doom. Shades of Sodom and Gomorah? Three grass-fringed pits bear testimony to the anger of the gods. Gingerly, I peer down one of them—it is dark, the overwhelming dark of a bottomless crevice. 'When you look into the abyss, the abyss also looks into you!' the words of Fredrick Nietzche jump out of nowhere.

Another eighty-degree climb through fragrant *brahmakamals* takes us to Kelua Vinayak, where, by tradition, all pilgrims carry a fifty-kilo statue of Ganesh around the platform for good luck.

Ahead in the cloud-snagged mountains are the bleak caves of Balpa Sulera where it is said the exhausted queen gave birth to a child in that ill-fated yatra. Others believe that the rains washed the straws from the cave where she gave birth into the Nandakini, rendering its waters unclean.

Fact and fiction merge into each other like the swirling mists. Yet to this day the waters of this river are not used for oblations at any temple in Garhwal.

Womenfolk in traditional wear participate in a religious festival in Wan village

Ram Singh, an eighteen-year-old schoolboy from Wan, showing unusual enterprise, has built a couple of rough rock shelters for the odd wanderer who dares come so far. For twenty rupees he rents them out.

'The Balpa Regency is on American Plan,' mutters my companion, 'tea included!'

With no place to pitch a tent, all at once, the work of the Great Sculptor is at hand. His sub-aerial tools of water, ice wedges, glaciers, snow, hail, sleet and rain together shatter the might of the mountains.

At dawn, I look up the scraped cliff and quarried stone and realise our destination is at hand. The raindrops at our feet turn to ice on frozen stone. This is the 'Ocean of Rocks'—Shailsagar.

Up a couple of zigzags and we are at Roopkund, completely exhausted. The four-horned ram must travel a little further to Homkund, 'the lake of fire sacrifice', before being set free. It finds its way, unaided, to the summit of Mount Trishul. This year the lake looks very small, its size varying with the warmth of each monsoon; often you'll meet trekkers arguing about the size of the lake. Don't worry! Both will usually be right.

Along the icy-edge are the skeletal remains of that fateful Raj Jaat Yatra. But the clouds triumph once again. The lake freezes over—hiding its dark secret for another time. ●

The Man Who Would be King

Devprayag, at the confluence of the Bhagirathi and Alaknanda rivers

Along the riverbed under the trees
I find the tracks.
In the fragrant grass I find the tracks
In the remote mountains I find the tracks
No more hidden than my nose.

Lost in the mountains, crouched in the swirling mists of a remote valley along the Bhagirathi River, thirty kilometers before Gangotri is the lesser-known destination Harsil.

Bouncing along an eyeball-rattling road, it had been a hard coming. Then, out of the incessant rain, below the sacred ranges, enveloped in a fine haze lay this thumbnail township. As the veil of mist lifted, it revealed rugged mountains laced with boulder-strewn rivers above which the hills were chequered with lonesome villages. The moody mountains looming out of the wintry thunderclouds, the sheer sweep of blossoming apple and peach orchards, the dusting of the wildflowers seemed like snow in the pale light of dawn. There is something of the eternal in the Himalayan snow, or perhaps something as close as we may ever glimpse.

Three mountain torrents rush down the slopes pursued by unseen demons. In one great burst, the glacial-born torrents of the Hari Ganga, the Neel Ganga and the Gupt Ganga merge into one.

A growing sense of what we've lost in Uttarakhand rode with me—as we drove along the gentle river, northward bound. We are told, over a thousand villages have been abandoned by the inhabitants. The splendid treeline, set against an azure sky, buoyed my spirits until we reached Sukhi Top as the sudden climb threatened to kill the engine.

Nearby, a stone's throw away, across the frothing waters are the proud remains of a mansion. Its curious architecture has never made it to the pages of any glossy magazine, it remains unsung though this blend of wood and stone has withstood the ravages of Time for over 150 years in the seismic-prone region of Uttarkashi.

Raja Wilson's home in Harsil

Right: Pioneer, shikari, timber merchant, Raja Wilson or Pahari Wilson of Harsil

Extreme right: Sangrami

Spurning the opprobrium of the Raj, he chose a life in the high mountains, where he could tune in, drop out and paddle his own canoe. Here he struck gold at the end of the rainbow by falling in love with the beautiful Sangrami or Gulabi, the pretty daughter of the drummer of Mukba village. Over the years, she became his good luck charm, his pot of gold in the remote wilderness! But that's another tale from another time ...

Walking up the Neel Ganga, I see the distant slopes covered in white. The glory of these stupendous ranges has, over the years, beckoned climbers to scale the summits that pierce the sky as far as the eye can see.

Nudging against the forests at 9,000 feet, the dark corduroy mounds of potato fields cover entire hillsides. How we take this humble tuber for granted today! Just three hundred years ago, it had not even touched the shores of Europe. In the hills, we owe its beginnings to the Irish freebooters, who brought it here after they saw its use as a buffer against famine in Ireland.

I drive away, leaving behind the immortal river.

The road was rough; potholes had torn great chunks off its scarred face, and tried to swallow up

While modern cement-concrete structures fell like ninepins on a dark autumn night in October 1991, this took it all. Around the house, the fading patterns of an abandoned garden are still visible.

Yes! This was once someone's home—far away from the world's maddening strife.

For this was home to a man who came to be known as Raja Wilson—the man who *was* a king in spirit!

our taxi. Our driver, familiar with these conditions, nonchalantly swerved around the crater-pitted roads. The precipitous edge did little to intimidate him.

But my mind was occupied elsewhere. I did not want to miss again, not this time, the lost temples of Mukba in the Gangotri valley of Garhwal.

Just a few weeks ago, I chanced upon a picture in an old railway magazine from the Raj, of two Himalayan temples: one large and the other a small miniature. Dancers of long ago were frozen at the foreground, in their attempt to appease the angry gods. I must assure you that in an earlier wandering through the valley, I had chanced upon a lonely spire sticking out of the sands of the river. But in this yellowing print from 1860s, it was all too clear. And yet I knew that given the proclivity of those concerned, these temples too would hold their stony silence and remain half-buried in the sands of the river.

Execlensia pines crown the upper reaches of the Bhagirathi valley

Climbing up, past the hot springs of Gangnani, the road arches like an eyebrow etched into the face of a precipitous cliff of Darua Tope. How did the place get its name, no one knows and no one will tell. Perhaps it has something to do with the headiness, the giddiness or swooning caused by similar heights not too different from the effects of *daru*, the thunder lightning of the local brew.

Suddenly, rising clear above the whine of the engine, comes the swishing of the breeze, keen as a knife, to bring me back to the present as we enter the cool of the northern aspects of the mountains.

There is little that the scanty woods can do to relieve the utter nakedness of the ranges. Somehow the melancholy pines still manage to root themselves and cling on to the deep gorges where no man dare venture.

Baillie Frazer, a traveller in the early part of the nineteenth century exclaimed: 'We are now in the centre of the most stupendous Himalayan ranges, the loftiest and perhaps the most rugged mountains in the world.'

The chaos you see today was not always there. Even the much-maligned Gurkha invaders treated these holy places with due reverence. It is reported that when

Sheep rearing is a major source of sustenance in the hills

an avalanche destroyed the ancient Gangotri Temple, the Gurkha general, Amar Singh Thapa, had it built anew.

If you were to go by his letters to the King of Nepal, we find a man who was God-fearing. In his letter of 2 March 1815 intercepted by British intelligence, he pleads:

> Ever since you (the King of Nepal) confiscated the jagirs of the Brahmin, thousands have been in distress and poverty. Promises were made that they should be restored at the capture of Kangra, and the orders of this effect under the red seal were addressed to me.
>
> We failed, however, in that object and now there is universal commotion. You ought therefore assemble all the Brahmins and promise to restore their lands and property, in the event of your conquering and expelling the British; by these means many thousands of respectable Brahmins will put their prayers for your protection and the enemy will be driven forth.

But it was not fated to be. Just six months later, in the fall, the British confronted their adversaries at the Battle of Nalapani on Kalinga Hill in the valley of the Doon. A month later the Gurkha rout was complete.

Gangotri Temple built by Amar Singh Thapa and later renovated by the Maharaja of Jaipur

Later the Gangotri Temple was damaged in a landslide and it was in the early decades of the last century that it was restored by the efforts of the Maharaja of Jaipur.

In my wanderings, time and again, I find the lost temples of Mukba springing from the pages of history. In June 1860, James Hulme wrote:

> At Deralle, the highest of villages on the Ganges, I found Wilson's camp. It is the nicest camping ground with the village's noise and dust out of sight in the rear, the apricot trees a forming nice shade, with a carpet of fresh green beneath, and the river running close by. A few yards from my camp, half buried in the sands of the river, were three temples, two very small, and the other with a tower about 30 feet high.

And so they remain. I find no attempts have been made to excavate these glorious reminders of an age when Shaivism merged with Buddhism. Almost 200 years later no one will bring them to life again.

This tragic tale of apathy and neglect repeats itself all over the mountains. The muted prayers of the worshipper in that faded picture from long ago cannot move the gods. They continue to wait on the shores of oblivion in the years to come.

Come summer and modern-day invaders shall descend upon these mountains, clucking about like concerned hens, a peck here and a nibble there and they'll be off no sooner lunch is over.

I meet sixty-year-old Rameshwar Dutt Hatwal, who worked as a guide in his youth. He looks at a bend in the road where a departing car leaves a cloud of dust and says: 'The buggers won't even look back. *Khatam ho gaya!* (It's finished!) Not as much as a belch will you get out of them. What do they care!'

What's worse is that he's right! There are many who sing of the glories of the Himalaya forgetting that those who live here cannot eat snow!

The chimul or rhododendron bushes rush into bloom after snow-melt

Easy accessibility! For what's so good on paper, oftener than not, turns into a nightmare in reality. Our pilgrim destinations have become shanty towns. They were not meant for tourism. Traffic snarls, fumes, choked sewers and garbage are the sole signs of progress.

Enthralling treks to what were once mere specks on a map have been overrun by tourists. With no infrastructure to take the load, everything creaked and fell apart like a leftover from a third-grade movie set.

If you were to take a walk along the most pristine of trails, you'd find the ubiquitous 'noodles, chips and chai'. Please don't you mind the garbage that has nowhere to go!

'Greed replaces need and commerce goes askew!' says fifty-year old Prem Singh, a teacher in the local school.

Unfortunately, he has no ready reckoners for this tourist blight. Tribhuvan Singh Bhandari, in his mid-fifties, found he could not cut through the forest of red tape and opted for a tented colony—straight out of the *Arabian Nights*. In a voice tinged with anguish he says: 'If only we could stop all these buses before Lanka!'

When you come here next time, take a walk along the Bhagirathi, past Lanka, across the scary bridge 1,340 feet off the valley floor, where once pilgrim and mendicant were held in thrall by the sounds of *gang-naad* or the celestial music of the river so near its source, as it swept round a bend before plunging into a deep chasm down below.

No such luck awaits you and me. A lane, no less seedy than the one in the plains, leads to the portals of the shrine. A sea of bamboo, hessian, jute and tin latrines cannot mask the stench of bleaching power and DDT. Together they conspire to wipe out the gentle fragrance of the pines.

Down below, the lost temples of Mukba are the only sentinels of silence, content to lie buried in the sands of Time. ●

The Magic of Duirital

If you look into the waters, the water looks back at you

He came rolling along the moonlit forest floor like a feline dream, a handsome black-capped pine marten—perfectly groomed in a glinting high summer coat. For a moment he hesitated, paused, inclined his head and listened. Should he proceed? Was it safe? Not till he had sniffed the pine-scented air to make sure.

A twig snapped under my feet. In a twinkle, he was gone, consumed by a thicket of wild rhododendrons as he vanished into the dark.

It is as if a delicately painted page in a fairy-tale book had suddenly come to life and then, all too soon, closed once again. The forest, once more, was still.

I have often run away to Duirital, to get away from it all–to this emerald lake set in the heart of the inner Himalaya, reflecting one of the most stupendous panoramas in all of Garhwal: the Chaukhamba massif arrayed on the northern edge with mountains piled on mountains whose peaks pierce the clouds.

A hot coming I had of it—a four-kilometre perpendicular climb for the road head just above Ukhimath. The sun beat down mercilessly upon the valley.

As the sun begins to set behind the crumpled hills, I am upon the lake, dotted by a solitary, sturdy dak bungalow. Much is to be said about the spots the old colonials chose to put these abodes all over the hills; I have found them in the most unlikely places. This spot was frequented by one of Garhwal's earliest commissioners, a J.H. Batten, whose administration lasted for a full twenty years, from 1836 to 1856; he had seen every nook and cranny in the area. On one visit here he was touched:

> The day I reached here it was snowing and young trees were laid prostrate under the weight of snow, the lake was frozen over to a depth of about two inches.
>
> There was no human habitation, and the place looked like a veritable wilderness. The next morning

Duirital near Ukhimath was a favourite of the early Britishers in Garhwal

Facing page: En route to the glacial lake of Roopkund

when the sun appeared, the Chaukhamba and many other peaks extending as far as Kedarnath seemed covered with a new quilt of snow, as if close to hand.

The whole scenery was so exquisite that one could not get tired of gazing at it for hours. I think a person who has a subdued settled despair in his mind would all of a sudden unexpectedly feel a kind of bounding and exalting cheerfulness which will be imparted to his frame by the scenery of Duirital.

What melancholic thoughts bothered Batten? No one will ever know. But the place does lift the spirits from the temporal to the eternal. That anyway is why I too have come to this citadel of calm.

Off the beaten track, the lake attracts few 'tourists'—so I've come armed with a dog-eared volume of Thoreau's Walden, to look for the healing balm of its magical waters. Of course, pragmatic science would have us believe these lakes are just glaciers left behind at the end of the Ice Age. I look for answers across the lush meadows ending in a mirror-like surface—reflecting an eternity of clouds and blue space.

Shades of science and mysticism ripple and shift like mirages on the tranquil surface of the waters. As we look into them, perhaps there is a reflection of who we really are!

Later, setting out along the lip-edge of the lake, I sight a young boy, astride the trunk of a dead tree fallen in the waters. Statuesque, he stands, fishing rod in hand, waiting for the fish to bite. Suddenly he whips out the line. He examines it. With an audible sigh, he flings the fingerling back into the lake.

Wads of tadpoles scurry off in fright, dimpling the waters.

'Go!' he says to the fish adding, 'Grow up soon! I will be back again.'

Lost in spirals of my own thoughts, I walk on along the cobbled path. At a bend in the shore, the pine martens are back. They dart to the waters, perhaps for a sip. But it was not to be; a mischievous tribe of black langurs decide to have some fun. And the pine martens vanish into the privacy of the forest.

As the sun sinks in the west, the stars begin their solitary vigil of the mountains. A breeze sweeps the surface of the lake, it is time to retreat to the warmth of the cabin to light a fire and delve into Thoreau's musings:

The calm water of Duirital mirrors the sky

Facing page: Gangotri glacier calves and gives birth to the Ganga

> A lake is the landscape's most beautiful and expressive feature. It is earth's eye; looking into which the beholder measures the depth of his own nature ... Sky water. It needs no fence; nations come and go without defiling it. It is a mirror which no stone can crack, whose gilding Nature continually repairs; no storm, no dust, can dim its surface ever fresh – a mirror which all impurity presented to it sinks, swept and dusted by the sun's hazy brush.

Outside, the wind whispers as an owl complains to the elements. I read on:

> I want to go and live away by the pond, where I shall hear only the wind whispering among the reeds ... But my friends ask what I will do when I get there. Will it not be employment enough to watch the progress of the seasons?

At dawn, cloaked in mist and morning clouds, the Banderpoonch massif rears like the sun from the shores of a lake, fed by its underground springs whose water is host to the denizens of the nearby forest, another day has begun. I tear myself away. It is time to get back to the world of civilisation ...

The last lines of my book ring clear in my ears: 'The light which puts out our eyes is darkness to us. Only that day dawns to which we are awake. There is more day to dawn. The sun is but a morning star.'

Spirits refreshed, I return from Garhwal's Walden Pond. ●

Chandrashila

Chandrashila – horoscopes fluttering in the wind

Chandrashila is the highest peak in the Inner Himalaya

There lies in Garhwal, Chandrashila—the highest peak in the inner Himalaya. It is a bleak, rock-strewn place, perched atop a crag. And if you look down, far, far below along the distant road you'll see the villages of Garhwal. Simple structures of mud, earth, slates, and weathered wood bunched together against the slopes as if for comfort.

The faint shadow of an invisible line plays through the speckled shadows of a coniferous forest—it is the only trace of the road travelled on just a few hours ago. But ah! The deodars—those trees of the gods, a close cousin of the Cedars of Lebanon, celebrated by writers of yore. 'The righteous shall grow like a cedar in Lebanon,' says the Psalmist. In the Bible, Isaiah used them to illustrate the goodness of God, in that he gave his people shelter from the scorching sun by planting 'in the wilderness the cedar'.

How did the deodar get to the Himalaya? No one knows, but a tale is told of how the first cedar made it to Europe. It began with an old Frenchman wandering the Holy Land. He picked a little seedling near the celebrated grove and on the stormy voyage home, when water stocks were depleted, each passenger on board was doled out just half a glass of water. This kind soul loved his seedling, sharing his meagre ration with his mate. The tree survived, while he had a close brush with death! With great aplomb, it was taken to the Jardin de Plantes, where it soon grew into a noble tree.

To its shade trudged the old and infirm, from a nearby prison the prisoners peeped out at its foliage, and then, when it was about 100 years old, it was cut down to make way for a railway line.

Tungnath's lonely eminence is a beacon to the wanderer

However, in the high mountains of Garhwal, the deodars prosper and given half a chance may they continue to flourish!

Ukhimath, the winter residence of the priests of Kedarnath, is a small town but the road passes it by, hurrying on to the canopy of green jungle visible at a distance. This then is the last bastion of the trees.

In this remote corner of the Nanda Devi sanctuary one can get some idea of how things would have been if they had been left alone. The mighty oak feathered and festooned with moss and ferns; wiry birch; pine and rhododendron and the forest floor, a carpet of slippery grass.

Maybe this is how the early commissioners of Garhwal found Duggalbetta. They built themselves an imperial bungalow. It sits squarely, comfortable as if in an armchair, facing the eternal snows, painted pink like some rare orchid mounted in an emerald sea of green. Someday it shall be a memory that'll hold your spirit. A vision of childhood spent in a dream.

And if you're tired give yourself up to the comforts of the Raj. Night comes quickly in the mountains and all is quiet but for the occasional nightjar.

As I snuggle up for the night, a blood-curdling shriek of a tormented soul rents the opaque darkness. Jumping out of bed, I grope for my boots and a torch. Clutching the torch, Narain Singh, the chowkidar, just smiles at me.

'Everyone jumps up like you ji' he mumbles, 'it is just the owls out again. Don't worry!'

Yes! The sirens of the night like the forest eagle-owl are aboard. Many fables, tales, stories and legends have made all the ages shudder with unreasonable horror at 'the Devil Bird'. A perfection of natural devices, this bird has a massive head, cruel beak, eyes almost popping out the disc of feathers in which the eyes are set and a tuft of feather atop its head—features designed, essentially, to impress the timorous.

For it is only at night that its majesty appears, as the great eyes collect whatever light tinctures the darkness, much like a night-vision device. Its alchemy is strength, furtiveness, brazenness, daring and a spirit of real enterprise: a lethal combination, which gives the owl an ability to rough it out in any weather. Of course the owls grow and prosper.

White and black and brown descends the forest eagle-owl, out on the prowl for the lone jackal, young barking deer, hares, lizards, or snakes. Often driving through the mountains at night, you will see a burst of feathers at a trickle on a culvert as the car slows down at the bends. Just a flurry of white-and-black-and-brown!

The calm water of Duirital—mirror to the sky

Even on a bad day, the rat was not born that a good owl would not carry off to its perch for supper. He is busy tonight with some rats, and tomorrow he has an appointment with some rundas (those mouse-hares, which are neither hares nor mouse!) May this natural venture flourish! With this thought, you drift off to the land of dreams.

Abruptly above Chopta the trees vanish, as if some unseen hand had taken a ruler and drawn a straight line across the face of the mountain. This is

the treeline and on its margin is the omnipresent chai shop. These watering holes provide more than food and sustenance to the weary band of travellers. Now, out of the smoke, like an apparition emerges Gopal Dutt Maithani. He greets us like long-lost brothers.

'To Tungnath?—You too! To have your horoscope done?'

Horoscope? Why? I wonder.

'Well! The priests are called "Friends of the Stars" and can cast great horoscopes and nativities.' He explains, adding: 'But even I can foretell you need a cup of tea.'

'Did you know that it was in Chandrashila that Ravana performed his austere tapasya? This is where he got the divya astra (divine weapons) from the gods!' he tells me.

I have no reason to doubt him. It is that kind of a place.

Where you know that man and his matters perish. Only the mountains are forever. ●

Baadis: The Flower Children of Garhwal

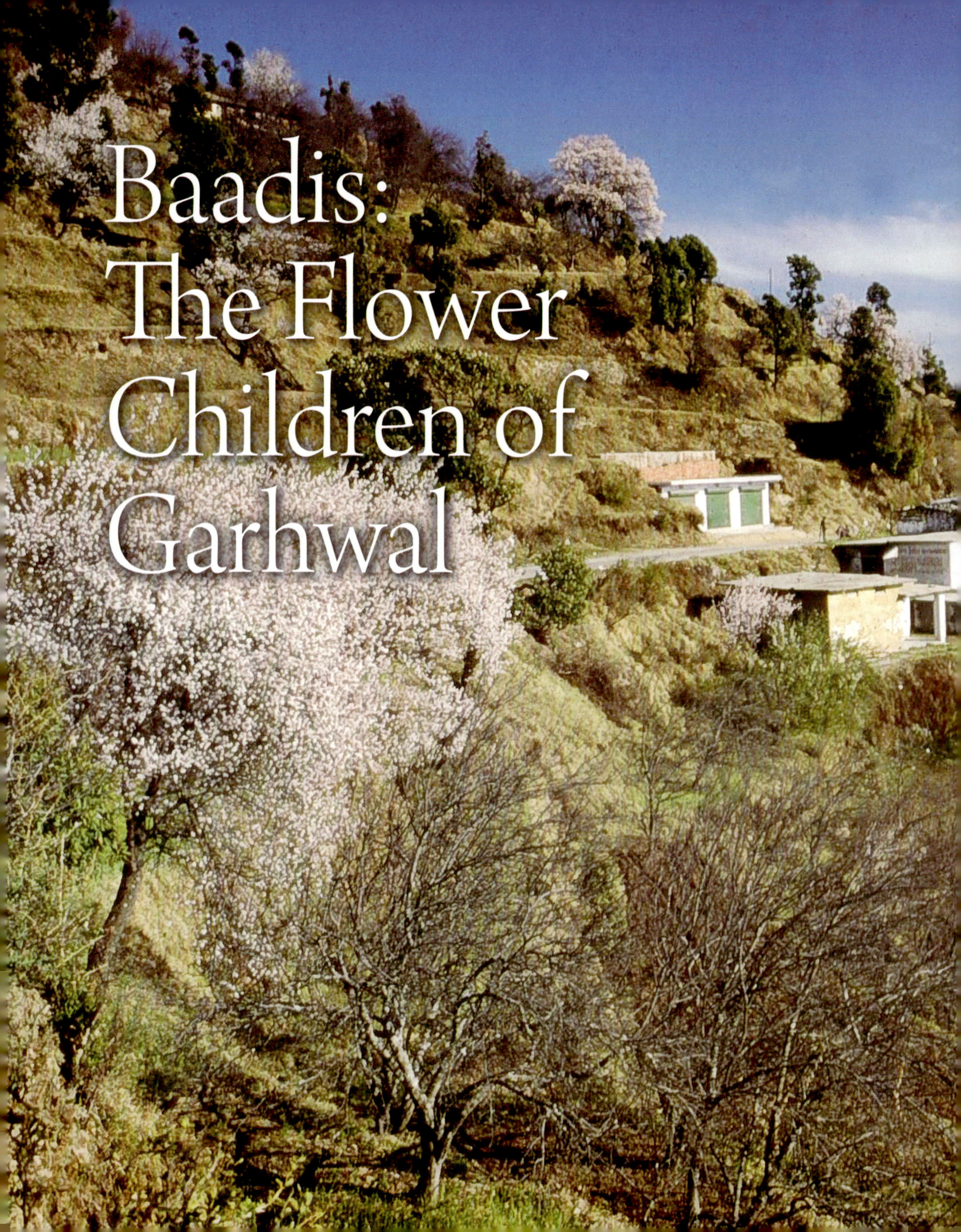

Apricot blossom-crested village in Garhwal

I can hear them long before I see them. Voices that rise clear over the erratic spluttering of our prehistoric bus. Carried by the breeze, the steady beat of a drum mingled with the tinkle of *ghungroos* reaches my ears.

A smile wraps itself on my co-traveller as she too senses the unvoiced question.

'Songsters, like gypsies you know… like the flower-children of the 1960s!'

'Out in the middle of nowhere?'

'Oh yes! The *baadis* are the real songsters of Garhwal.'

The sun climbs over the distant peaks as luminous vapours turn wrinkled mountains into orderly, creased, manicured terraces. Fields of amaranth, the autumnal *chaulai* or *ram-dana* make the fields blush crimson at dawn as they flirt with the playful teasing of the errant wind. The lush green grass has been stored away to fade in clumps of haystacks like blond wigs to cover the balding walnut trees. I am a wanderer here, just passing through this remote village in Khaspatti in the Garhwals.

On the farthest slopes, almost outside the main cluster of the village, lives Girdhari. A *baadi,* who like his ancestors, is a folk musician, historian and an instant bard. An unwritten law, part of a perverse tradition has it that all artisans must live only on the lowest slopes of the villages. A rubble-strewn path debouches on his simple hut etched into the base of the mountain.

A gigantic five-ton slate roof winks at the sun. Chimneyless roofs force the grey-blue smoke to pour out of the solitary door. Is it a fault in design?

Left: *Baadis*—the folks singers of Garhwal

Right: Folk dancers carry on a long tradition of joy and happiness in the Garhwal Himalaya

Or is it the occupation of the land by the Gurkhas for two and a half decades? If folklore and proverbs are something to go by, then it is the latter. You wouldn't want your enemy sliding down the chimney! Would you?

And I find that 'Gurkhyani' is an expression used by the old-timers to describe impossibility or an attitude where having glugged down all the milk at night, one was to insist on having curds at breakfast!

On hearing my tumbling down the path, Girdhari peeps out of the doorway, hookah cupped in his hands, rubbing the smoke from his watery eyes. Seeing the tape-recorder slung over my shoulder, he dashes back into the hut, slamming the door in my face. What's up? Could I have done something wrong? All I have for an answer is a one-legged crow trying to land on a bare medlar tree and missing. Far away, a lonely eagle floats effortlessly in the invisible eddies of the wind.

The door bursts open. Swathed in smoke with a tinkle of ankle bells, she steps out. She's a swarthy woman, confident of herself, the mainstay of this family and the backbone of its existence. No clairvoyant is needed to find out who had the final word in the family. Without much ado, she gently places a baby in a basket, an improvised hammock, and sits down to adjust her ankle bells. Girdhari too steps out, the hookah has been transformed as if by magic into a drum. He caresses the taut skin with his long fingers.

'Which song would you like babuji?'

'Anything!'

One last time, he strums the drum and then the dance begins. Their vibrant voices flow in a crystal stream, rising in joy and passion. The magic turns the plain housewife into a dancer; an inspired one, who throws her head, taps her feet and sways till the very hair on her head seems to come to life. Something more than an electric spark jumps between them and back again.

Dhols carry on a fast-vanishing ancient tradition

Is it love? Or are the muses hovering here? I pinch myself remembering that one must be careful in this land of the *aacharis,* the ever-playful mountain fairies that are reputed to whisk away the lost wanderer. A soulful ballad has it that Surju Kunwar, a warrior of old, once sat on a ridge playing on his fife, when the naughty fairies carried him off to their land of eternal afternoons. He never returned!

The dancers look at me. Did they read my thoughts? The tape recorder answers not. It is content to be a mute witness to this symphony in the mountains, trapping the melodies of these Homeric bards in the backwoods.

The first song is of love in a land where all young men join the male exodus to the parched lanes of the plains in search of livelihood. In the shimmering heat of these places far from home, memories of the peaceful mountains cloud many a misty eye.

By now, the boundary wall looks like a grandstand. Ensconced atop is a jostling group of children playing truant from school. But they are easily forgiven for what could be a better reason to have a holiday?

Pure envy gets the better of a lean bystander and he leers at the *baadis*: 'Yes! Yes! Keep it up you'll make it to the Bombay-cinema one day!'

The dancer stops. A cloud of contempt crosses her face. A hush descends as the crowd gapes expectantly. Arms akimbo, she glowers in outrage.

'A crow never changes its mantle! Does it!' she yells. The gathering bursts into laughter as the bully's bluff is called. The moment passes. The lean and hungry loafer slinks up the narrow path back

Drummers of Garhwal carry forward an old tradition

to the village. His grumblings are lost as the next song begins:

O Darling in the mountains, love of mine,
Lost in the plains for you I pine.
The playful breeze your locks will tease,
While I in the plains, other folks do please.
Your companions will greener pastures find,
While you alone the wheat will grind.
In the hills and valleys deep,
The doves in love-lorn laughter sweep,
While I lost in the plains....
Your friends in the paddy green,
While you alone the pots will clean.
While I lost in the plains.

The toddler in the basket raises a shrill cry in protest. Feeding time. In a single movement, she scoops up the babe and cuddles him. Fled is the magic and the housewife returns.

'Will he too become a *baadi*?'

'No! No! Too much prejudice! He'll go to school and become "something"!'

It is time to move on.

Girdhari insists on helping me up the rocky path, past the village on to the dusty road to await the stuttering bus. But I will never forget the dark unfathomable *baadi* from the mountains or the warmth of his sandpapery hands as he grasped mine for one last goodbye.

Was he destined to be the last of the flower children of Garhwal?

I can still hear the old music pounding and sailing into the sky, and feel the mystery of legends whispered to my young ears about the origin of those songs.

I can still recall the dance of the people who believed their ways were the only ways. ●

Travels in the Bhyundar Valley

Ghagharia—doorway to the Valley of Flowers

My eyes are blinded by the brilliant colours of a valley that wears a quilt of finely embroidered flowers. I stand and stare, wide-eyed and speechless, at flowers of every imaginable colour and hue. The air is so saturated with scent that clouds of fragrance, wafted by a gust of Himalayan breeze, storm my senses.

'*Kyoon sahib … kya hua*?' (What's happened sahib?) The robust voice of our guide intrudes. The spell is broken. But the magic lingers, working a different kind of spell this time.

'*Yeh hai* Bhyundar Valley!'

The Valley of Flowers. Lying at a height of 4,115 metres, snug in the upper Himalaya; a valley many travellers have written about, each influenced by his own sensations, his own experience. No human could have created such a paradisiacal garden. In fact, to my mind, none of the famed gardens of the Mughul emperors—Nishant, Shalimar, Chashma Shahi, could match this natural garden in visual splendour.

One cannot help but believe the awed villagers who, with a hint of fear in their voices, whisper that at night the mountain fairies tend this garden by the light of a million glow-worms. A garden at the gateway of Heaven that is watered by its own sacred fount—the Pushpa Ganga, or the 'River of Flowers' which in autumn is abloom with over a thousand varieties of exotic Himalayan flowers.

Autumn is the best time to be in the Valley of Flowers. We set out one chilly morning along the road towards Tehri. The nearby slopes sprout orchards of peach, plum and apricot. The ride is smooth to the district headquarters of the hill-district of Tehri-Garhwal. We have been here before and drive on to Srinagar, the capital of the old Garhwal Kingdom—the land of fifty-two forts. The dull grey silt brought down by innumerable flash floods give this bustling town a sombre look.

We are engulfed by cloudburst. During the height of monsoon, some of the sudden downpours can bring much rain in an hour. As we inch our way through the deluge, a bold wayside signboard warns: 'Landslide active. Drive at your own risk!' Seconds later, as if on order, the mountain-face moves down to obliterate the road. Each time, the road moves further back into the folds of the mountain. With the road gone for the umpteenth time, we wait at the edge of the landslide.

Six hours and four bulldozers later, a fresh path is carved out of the gelatinous mud, allowing us, along with a cavalcade of other stranded vehicles, to continue the journey to Karnaprayag. According to legend, the great Karna was cremated here on

Govindghat was extensively damaged by the floods

Facing page: Taking a break with wildflowers

Pilgrims en route to the Sikh shrine of Hemkund

the palm of Krishna's hand. The road rises sharply to Joshimath, a Shangri-La sheltered by the towering peaks.

A short drive to Govindghat and from here one will have to walk. A suspension bridge spans the river. A shaggy animal crouches at the entrance to the bridge. We stop. Not too sure. It lifts its head—the famous Himalayan mastiff, the ancestor of all mastiffs. In winter, it guards the flocks of sheep against marauding leopards and wolves, themselves not being easy prey because of their formidable size, and the thirteen-centimetre spiked iron collar they normally wear.

'Its ancestors must have been a bear!' mutters a lanky pilgrim and turns to us to say, 'It's best you get a fresh start in the morning. The climb to Ghagharia can take up to ten hours!' Road-weary as we were, he did not have to say much to convince us.

Next morning we begin to walk up the steep sixteen-kilometre path to Ghagharia, common to Hemkund and the Valley of Flowers. In the mid-June calamity of 2013, the Dwari bridge over the Pushpawati Ganga had been swept away and a makeshift wooden bridge stands in its stead. Majestic mountains topped with sun and snow glisten in their pristine glory. Against a frieze of silver-birch trees, is the small village of Bhyundar with a single chai shop.

Soon, we are joined by a group of pilgrims on their way to the highest Sikh shrine of Hemkund. Most have seen many winters and only faith keeps them going on this hilly trek.

The cheerful song of the whistling thrush invites us to quicken our pace, but at our approach the bird flies off into the woods. Its plaintive anthem fades. Legend has it that Krishna fell asleep one warm afternoon near a brook and while he slept, a playful boy walked off with his celestial flute. On awaking, he noticed that the flute was gone and in anger he turned the little boy into a bird; but by then the naughty one had learnt the music of the gods, only stopping now and then (as the whistling thrush does!) when he forgets the right note.

Tourists at a tented colony

The sun has ended its journey and we are all more than content to give ourselves to the hospitality of the shrine at Ghagharia. At the crack of dawn, the stars seem to have come closer to the earth. The valley is still shrouded in a low mist. Slowly, the stars are extinguished one by one and the sun begins to scale the mountains. We enter through a long belt of rhododendron that in summer will stain the mountains crimson with their blooms. The mist lifts to reveal glaciers across the Pushpa Ganga, making progress low and slippery.

Suddenly we are there. I see the valley christened by Frank Smythe in 1931 as 'The Valley of Flowers', spread over eighty-seven square kilometres. A weariness born of travel creeps upon us. A tired Himalayan poppy hangs in sleep on a rocky crag. Seven silent streaks of quicksilver cascade off the ancient rocks to water this quiet Eden. Aged glaciers remain the sentinels of the flowers. The air is chilled. At my feet the flowers are encrusted with pearls. Indeed it is impossible to walk a single step without crushing a flower!

At dawn, the sun steals over the lush meadows and flashes blue light up these austere heights. One feels like a wanderer from another planet and the words of an ancient Sanskrit poet echo in my ears: 'In a hundred ages of the gods I could not tell thee of the glories of the Himalayas!'

The grave of botanist Joan Margaret Legge has a new tombstone with the inscription: 'Feb 21, 1885–July 4, 1939, I will lift mine eyes unto the hills from whence cometh my help.' She lies here amongst the flowers she loved so much. Feeling like an intruder, I place a nosegay for a second time on her grave and tiptoe away from this shrine in God's own garden ... promising to return once again.

Just a five-kilometre climb up from Ghagharia and you are at Lokpal. At 14,000 feet, the air is thin—sucking the very breath of life out of you. Comes another sledgehammer blow, stunning the senses. All is white. Blinding white. The glacial lake of

Carried after the wedding in a palanquin, a Garhwali bride takes a break

Lokpal and the seven snow-driven peaks that tower jaggedly to pierce the skies.

Clinging to the grass, we lie sprawled at the edge of a crystal lake—winded and tired—yet strongly exhilarated, seeing the mist creep and crawl in the valleys down below. We are alone up here and the moment is lodged for eternity in our minds.

'*Sat Sri Akal*!' The sacred invocation to their gurus echoes in the mountains. Our fellow travellers have caught up with us. Old and young, rich and poor, clamber up the cobbled paths with walking sticks, on piggy back and on mules as young mothers shield babies from the icy blast. A strong porter carries an old pilgrim in a wicker basket. For a moment he puts it down and wipes the sweat on a tattered sleeve. The wind claws at him. The basket stirs, 'Hurry up! Will you?' a voice yells at him.

Khem Singh is not amused. He throws a baleful glare at the basket. A frown furrows his brow; a cloud comes over his face.

'Never! Never again will I make this forty-mile trip again!' he mutters. But he will, poor Sisyphus, twice a week for four months in the year during the tourist season. The 200 rupees will add to the meagre income from the narrow, weather-plagued fields of this village down below.

Lokpal is the god of directions and the eight sub-divisions of the compass are guarded by *lokpals* astride their beautiful elephants. Thus, Kuber, the lord of wealth prefers the north, while Indra, the lord of thunder and rain chose the east.

Another legend has it that Lakshman meditated on the edge of the lake a long time ago. A crumbling temple marks the spot. Treading along the withered edge, past the ruined cairn, a figure catches my eye, I step closer. Momentarily, the stones come alive. Our eyes lock. The other alcove is empty. Have the vandals been at work? No answers.

Ambling up to me, another strapping pilgrim exclaims: 'Wonderful... isn't it? To be here at Hemkund—where Guru Govind Singh meditated in his last incarnation.'

At the end of every valley stands a lofty summit

'True,' I murmur. A rare treat to be in a place doubly blessed. Some distance away, I see a shepherd frozen in thought. At my approach, he springs to life.

'Where is the flock?' I ask.

'Grazing down there ... somewhere ... Do you know goats are smart creatures? They can really take care of themselves—besides each one has nine brothers!'

Nine brothers?

'Well, four to carry it about, two on the head to protect it, two as ears to fan it and one little brother behind to flick away the flies. Goats are well looked after. No? But tell me, are you too looking for *apsaras*?'

I'm stumped. '*Apsaras*? Celestial nymphs? The heady stuff of ancient dream. Up here?'

'Oh yes!' he says with a twinkle in his eye. 'My grandfather once told me of how when he was young, he stole up the mountain one moonless night and had a glimpse of them gamboling in the crystal waters. And I too come up here—but so far, no luck! Do you think they'll turn up someday?'

'Maybe ... who can tell?'

Leaving our garrulous shepherd to his solitary vigil, I move on. A blissful silence reigns. The silver sheen of the peaks is mirrored in the waters. There is something about the place, an impalpable mysticism.

In a workshed near the new gurdwara, pilgrims huddle like penguins, swapping stories around a fire with steaming glasses of tea. A glass finds its way to me. It is sweet and comforting. But Khem Singh, our porter, beckons from behind a rock where he draws on the tea.

'Oh! I'll never forget,' he tells me, 'I was working on the road to Badrinath. Yes! The charge exploded, I rushed up to the freshly opened rock face and gaped into a cave. A man wrapped in ochre stared at me before he vanished into thin air. And sahib, those piercing eyes have haunted me forever.'

Hemkund shrine on the edge of Lokpal Lake—doubly blessed

© Ambika Singh

The serrated ridges of the many folds of the Himalaya at dusk

Wiping the cold damp off his forehead, he walks back to the wicker basket. A small pica, a combination of mouse-and-hare, surfaces from under the rocks and scurries away. What is the world's smallest hare doing up here among the tallest mountains? I wonder.

The clouds envelope the seven peaks and pass through them gently like ghosts turning up on the other side. It's time to return. A sense of camaraderie ties total strangers together as they help each other down the 3,000 steps. Ahead, Khem Singh has halted again. The basket is empty. The old pilgrim, on hands and knees, hair trailing in the breeze, is crawling towards an overhang.

'Altitude sickness?' I venture.

'Ha! Nothing like that! Pure vanity. The old woman wants one of those *brahmakamals*!' he says, pointing to a cluster of large flowers on a ledge.

I step closer mulling why some folks pluck wildflowers? As if in answer to my unvoiced question, her wrinkled face cracks into a smile.

'Son, I've heard that the pollen of this flower was used by Draupadi for her wonderful skin. Don't worry. I won't be back here in a hurry—not in this lifetime at least—and the flowers shall bloom again. No?'

The logic is deafening. It gets the better of me, setting at rest my ecological concerns. Plucking a flower, the velvety petals crumble to the touch, the pollen falls in my hands. I rub it on my face. Nothing happens.

Peals of laughter emanate from the basket, as if to say: Why? What did you expect—miracles?

I move back to the cobbled path. Khem Singh smiles at me. We swing back to the beaten path winding its way past the misty waterfalls of Ghagharia.

Above, the peaks are lost in swirling mists. Are the nymphs back again for a dip? •

Haridwar: Along the Ganga

Har-ki-Pauri in Haridwar at sundown has a spectacular Ganga aarti

A hundred eyes stare at me. Unblinking, a peacock fans his tail in the rain. A soft cathedral light filters through the canopy of the Siwalik forest. The whispering breeze tells no tales of the city ahead. Crouched in the mist, Haridwar, along the banks of a mighty river, awaits you.

It's here that the glacier-fed Ganga ends her tortuous journey through the mountains, debouching onto the vast plains of India. Her silt-laden waters betray no memories of a majestic birth higher up in the snow-mantled mountains. Of course, sometimes, she plays truant and her swollen waters flood the teeming cities lining her 1,400-mile path to the Bay of Bengal.

For the believer there is no place of pilgrimage more sacred than the river. To partake of her waters is to be released from the endless cycles of rebirth. Often, occasionally, the hordes descend and stampedes occur—a phenomenon for which there are many ideas but no consensus. Indeed, Homo erectus *is* the real problem.

Descending the steep steps to the bathing ghats, you hurry along with the crowds which move about in clumps. The river flows on diverging spokes of light where the sun's rays bounce off its glistening surface. Peals of laughter resound across the morning air. Celebrations for a lifetime's desire fulfilled.

The place has always been a favourite of the gods. A legacy of names survive, variously known as Brahmapuri, Hari-ka-dwar, Ganga-ka-dwar or Kapila. Haridwar is the current favourite and anyway, who can unravel history's enigmas?

'What a mess we've made!' exclaims an elderly pilgrim. On an average day, the crush of pilgrims propels you on towards Har-ki-Pauri where you find yourself deposited under the ubiquitous Clock Tower.

Undeterred by the current, a boy feels his way for offerings thrown into the riverbed. With feline grace that would put any self-respecting cat to shame, he scoops one up, takes one look at it and flings it back. A dark cloud passes over his face. 'A defaced coin!' he exclaims, 'What is the world coming to? Mocking Mother Ganga?'

In reply, the fish shy away from his bleached feet.

Riparian activities along the upper reaches of the river—some 200 miles of its tortuous journey through the mountains—have been destroyed by the ravaging of the forests and the fish are all but extinct. Yet, in Haridwar, all life is sacred and the fish prosper. Pampered, they grow fatter by the day, as do a host of astrologers lining the path. In the sweltering heat, they wait for you.

Gaumukh glacier—the Ganga's icy origins

Facing page: Waiting for the gods

A squabble breaks out over a passing client—me. The resultant logic wanders down dubious lanes:

'Wasn't your grandfather too a fortune teller?' one mocks the other.

'Why not? And a great one at that!'

'Couldn't foretell what was going to happen to himself next? Could he? Remember the time the Maharaja threw him into the jail!'

Heady stuff this genealogical debate. I escape them, by the simple expedient of weaving my way through the narrow lanes. Crossing one of the bridges that span the river, I am back again at the water's edge. A frail collection of leaf-boats bob up and down, the remnants of someone's prayer: a charred wick, dab of camphor, a clump of jasmine and memories.

Does this bring me here?

For here in my childhood I saw—crowded ghats, chanting of prayers, abandoned palaces, tinkling bells, the scent of incense and the rush of the Ganga Canal. For when the place calls, I must go.

P.B. Cautley, a sodier-turned-engineer, dreamt up the Ganga Canal in the 1840s to banish the spectre of famine from the Doab, or the land that lies between the Ganga and Yamuna. But the directors of the East India Company were sceptical; the priests frowned, perceiving this as yet another attempt to control the holy river. He pacified them with the simple expedient of leaving a gap in the dam, using his personal funds to ensure that the waters flowed on unfettered.

Other obstacles lay in his path—more than thirty *billion* bricks were baked to build all the

Right: Prayers afloat petals flowing down the Ganga

Left: Lakshman Jhula built in 1927-29, opened to pilgrims in 1930

accompanying structures to go with the canal. A total of 103 bridges spanned the waters at each of the bathing ghats.

A tale has it that one day the Raja of Tehri woke up to find his personal ghat gone dry. The waters had been diverted into the canal. Requests to shift to an adjoining place for his prayers went unheeded. He went into a sulk, stalking off, muttering: 'My Ganga will come to me.'

Next morning, or so the tale goes, a flash flood upstream sent the waters lapping back to the old ghat again and did much to restore the raja's lost reputation.

Changes, more dramatic than this, are plain for all to see. The riotous din of the apartment builders, peddling dreams in this old-world place, add to the chaos. Cars zip through narrow lanes where the clippety-clop of tongas once sounded a lullaby. Youngsters careen around on flashy bikes. I move away towards the farther bank where, a long time ago, my father had taught me to step into the rushing current without being swept away. Just a touch of the magical waters and I am young again.

A light exists on the stairway to the Chandi Devi and Mansa Devi temples. A narrow and steep path climbs a hump crowned by temples on the opposite banks of the river, like two sentinels at the gorge.

Elaborate arrangements are made, especially on every twelfth year, when the planet Jupiter being in Aquarius and the sun enters Aries and the Maha Kumbh begins. Old records tell us that in 1819, 400 sepoys were crushed to death 'as every pilgrim struggled to be the first to plunge into the river at the propitious moment.' Later, during the Raj, the present ghat of sixty steps, 100 feet long, was built. Yet feelings continue to run high and each Kumbh Mela needs more special arrangements.

While resources have increased, the sheer weight of numbers has grown geometrically. By the time the paint is barely dry on bridges built for the last Kumbh, they are already too small.

Above the right bank of the river, a narrow lane barely four feet wide is lined with rows of shops selling trinkets. Sprouting out of walls, peepul trees strain to get a glimpse of the sky, which is all but lost in a maze of three-storey buildings. Here, Hiuen Tsang, the intrepid traveller from the seventh century, tarried a while in a place he called Mo-yu-lo. Today, there are rows of money changers, only too willing to change your crisp note for smaller coins. This eases the distribution of alms. Morality is not even a distant cousin of decency in the marketplace where the river of silver merges with the river of gold.

Around the ghats, people meditate and recite their prayers. Incense burns. Bells tinkle. Conch-shells sound. The marble walkway feels soft and slippery as I kneel. Eyes shut and head bowed, people pray.

A priest thrusts a camphor-edged flame. A profusion of hands caresses the flames. The sated cry of '*Jai Ganga Mai*' rises in the air to be lost in the boom of the river. Far away, the awkward call of the peacock calls an end to the day.

The devout shuffle away with a lifetime's desire fulfilled. Some may never return, but their ashes will. Haridwar is indeed that kind of place where past, present and future are woven tightly together in a single weave.

People thronging the Kumbh Mela at Haridwar

Though, of this I am sure, it'll take more than prayers to solve her problems. Little has changed here from the 1930s when Frank Smythe observed a group of pilgrims setting off for distant Badrinath:

> It was a cool still morning and already the path was thronged with pilgrims. They were an amazing assortment of men and women: fakirs, with wild, haggard, sunken faces and unkempt beards, clad only in a tiger-cloth, their bodies smeared with ashes, and others squatting like some bull-frogs on charpoys borne by sweating coolies, their women-folk plodding dutifully in the rear, carrying the family bedding, cooking-pots; queerest sight of all, little old men and women, so old it seemed impossible that life could persist within their fragile shrunken bodies, hunched uncomfortably in wicker baskets on the backs of the coolies. But most were on foot.

Almost a hundred years later, it's no different as I set off down the road to Haridwar. With tough determination, they venture on this pilgrimage, something sustains them; all seem to enjoy the pilgrimage, so their faces are intent, their minds set on the goal. They are not over-awed, too, by the dangers of the road; you can see this in their faces. City-bred folks, often find ourselves wondering what goes on in the minds of these simple folk, many of them from the remote parts of India.

Wonderment and faith must be the prime ingredients! Only then does the pilgrimage become an adventure. Unknown dangers lurk along the highway, the broad well-made path where the vehicles hurtle by; at any moment the gods, who hold the strings of fate, may unleash their wrath upon the hapless passer-by. To some it's just earthen pots filled with water, but to the pilgrim *this* walk along the highway is far, far more than just a walk to the banks of a holy river.

You'll find the pilgrims plodding along the way. Most are clad in white, with a pink scarf thrown across the shoulder, most casually, but here and there were splashes of vivid colour: old and young, feeble and infirm, plod, plod, plod. They pass by in thousands. And soon numbers are no more than a sequence of digits.

I sit in the shade of a boulder and wonder why? What is the force that impels them from their homes on the plains of northern India to Haridwar? Or is it a religious motive? It is something far more complex and indefinable.

'One carries the *kanwar* for two reasons—to thank God for fulfilling a wish, or to ask Him to let things be as they are!' says Satish Kumar, of Haryana. From what I saw, *kanwarias* are the most satisfied of people. Each gets a warm welcome at roadside camps organised by local organisations. Here they rest at night to give relief to their tired feet.

As Ram Bharose of Meerut puts it: 'The journey has its hazards yet nobody ever drops out half-way!'

'What if the water touches the ground?' I ask.

'It's rendered impure.'

Somewhere near Khatauli, Ram Bharose stops walking. Hot and puzzled. He wipes his brow, takes a swig of water and then intently walks on. I stride on the pathway to Har-ki-Pauri, the most pious place for the pilgrims. While some recite mantras, others fold their hands in prayer. A man sits in the silence of dawn, amid thousands of *kanwarias*. Perhaps this is real solitude in multitude. The community sits around him but he is alone. Sometimes he winces as an old blister on his feet is pricked afresh, but faith keeps him going. The rest does not matter.

Dawn breaks gently over the Himalaya

Haridwar draws devotees of all ages. Here in the world of religion, believers thrust their hands through its water. It has made it possible for all people to take nourishment from an ageless expression of human yearning for the eternal.

'It's so relaxing to walk on the banks of this great river,' says Shiv Singh, another intrepid walker.

During the time of pilgrimages Haridwar presents a scene of colourful activity. Along the bank, we pass a strange medley of saffron-clad figures, repeating in their garments the brilliant notes of the flame of the forest, which, in spring, paints the woods orange. These dusky hordes, a million strong, come from all parts of India to celebrate the famous Dikhanti festival, held every year on the first day of Baisakhi, the commencement of the Hindu solar year (March-April) which marks the day on which the Ganges first appeared on earth.

Har-ki-Pauri is also known as Brahmkund. It is believed if one takes a dip in the holy water, sins are washed away. From this very spot *kanwarias* will carry the holy water to their homes. The principal object of this festival is the Har-ki-Charan or bathing ghats with the adjoining temple of Gangadwara. The footprint of Vishnu is imprinted here on a stone led into the upper wall of the ghat and forms an object of special reverence. When the propitious moment arrives, each pilgrim with his eyes fixed on the mystic sign strives to be the first to plunge into a sacred pool.

On the western shore lies the city itself, with its succession of triple-domed temples and ghats. Among these temples only one deserves special mention—the temple of 'Maya-Devi' which is built entirely of stone and appears, gauging from the remains of ancient inscriptions, to date to the tenth or eleventh century. The principal image here is of the demons being vanquished by the gods.

There are some differences as to the goddess this image represents, some feel that it is actually 'Maya-Devi' as the image is locally known, while others assert that it is that of Durga.

But our carriers of holy Ganga water do not wait here. They are on their way, hurrying to their homes with holy water in grateful offering to the Lord of the Universe. And Time is rushing by! •

Himalayan Blossoms

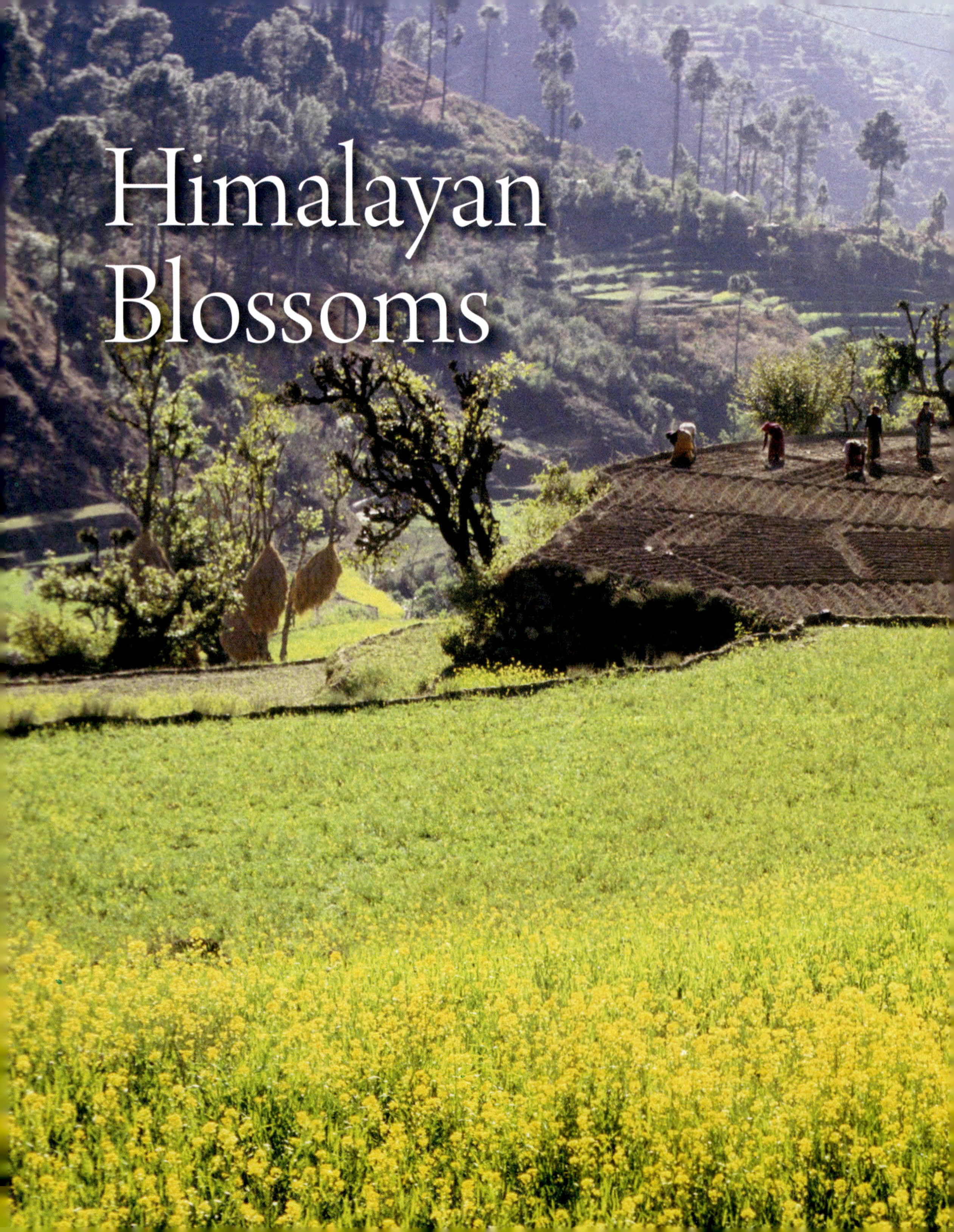

Field of ripening mustard frown upon the furrows of potatoes

A green hill with yellow flowers in a small school called Woodlands. Past the lyre tree, across a picket gate, a sombre man peering down at the little boy and he, all of ten years old.

'So you're the new volunteer? Are you? Can you find the yellow flower? Good luck!'

Assured a bounty of four-*annas* for each blossom, who needed convincing?

For him, the romance of wild flowers had just begun.

I was clambering up the hill, to look for the first flower of spring in the foothills of the Himalaya, not your common periwinkle, but butter-yellow blossoms. The hill was just another hill, maybe a little more crumpled than others with a dense canopy of oaks.

What a wonderful place for the eyes of childhood with daydreams of goblins and fairies! And what happened to the success of the first expedition?

It was rather easy. What flower or fairy can ever hope to hide from the keen eyes of childhood? Taking the short cut, he headed to the treasure trove of *phyunlis* (as the hill children call them), gathered as many as he could in his little hands. He was back to the sombre man, who knew much about flowers. Familiar hills seem to get higher as time passes by till one day you cannot climb hills any longer. Age, they say in the Garhwals, is but the grindstone of memory.

Dashing up the steps, two at a time, bursting through a solid oak door into the school office—a victor comes home with the spoils—a cascade of yellow on a baize-topped desk. Nothing on either side was said. Out of the bulging pockets, he drew his wiry spectacles, felt the petals one by one. Convinced they were real, he opened a drawer and out came his reward.

He took off, slid down the banisters with the good bitter fragrance of flowers on his hands and a cheery song in his heart. At last, he had the money to buy *the* kaleidoscope he had seen in the little shop near the Clock Tower in Landour Bazaar.

Lesson for the day: Money earned *honestly*—not bad at all.

Sometimes walking through the mountains of the Himalaya, if you pause to catch your breath besides a boulder, you too will wonder why many flowers prefer a crevice to grow in? Is it not harder on the roots? If you were to take the saxifrage, your typical lover of the rocks, notice how the members of this vast family flourish in stoniest soils. Their motto seems to be the tougher you are, the better it gets! Look closely at that rock face; it is so solid that no plant can ever

Bountiful rhododendrons line the forests above Chopta

Facing page: A peacock orchid or lady's slipper steals forth from the forest floor

General Winter's mantel of white cover the hills

hope to get any sustenance from it. Yet there it is—as real as you and me—alive and kicking on a dash of soil.

What keeps them going?

This Spartan existence on a thimbleful of soil is a miracle. Inside an invisible crack, hidden from a casual observer or an unobservant glance, but enough for the plant to prosper; brings echoes of our school choir:

Rock of Ages cleft for me,
Let me hide myself in Thee.

Yet another lover of the rocky soil is the oxalis or wood sorrel, its pinkish mauve flowers set like a jewel in a cluster of heart-shaped emerald leaflets. The hill folk call it the *khatta-metha* or the sweet-sour because of the mild acidity of its leaves. The cows love it but then their milk curdles easily. Often you'll find people basking in the sun, polishing the brass base of their hookahs with its leaves. If mistakenly, one happens to swallow the poisonous seeds of the *dhatura,* the juice of the plant is a good cure.

The sheep sorrel is a tough weed. It will grow on rocks, the walls of old houses, or in the soil of crumbling ruins that cannot support any other plant. The confetti-like pink and red flakes appear in the spring, but these too are acidic. On degraded slopes, after the quarriers have left, on hillsides most

exposed to the wind, among the grass and shrubs, you will find them taking root and restoring the verdure of the hills.

In the hills, the mist-laden rains are the oldest friends of the flowers. A sward of flowers and ferns cover the ground. Sprays of wild ginger are ablaze in all their glory.

At the end of the monsoon, watch out for the cobra lily with its protruding tongue, they creep forth silently across the mushy forest floor. The snake-like imitation is so real that neither bird nor beast dares come near it. When the plant goes into seed, you can rest assured the rains are well and truly over. Yet look closely; that pale mauve is the lady's slipper hugging the ground, tender and vulnerable to even your passing shadow. Pity they bloom so briefly. Tougher is the lady's mantle looking like a crochet spread out to dry in the sun.

When Winter begins to marshal his troops of sleet and snow, there is still time to rejoice like the convolvulus' trumpet flowers. Knowing that autumn in the mountains is at best a brief affair, it is always found in a great hurry to be climbing over all things, both big and small, astride its own silver-downed harp-like strings.

The crowning glory of all the wild flowers is the *feinkamal*, with a pale tint from blossoming in the shade of the eternal snows. A legion of romance and legends spring all around it. In the Himalaya they say, once upon a time, there lived an old miser.

Frank Smythe's famed Valley of Flowers is now a protected sanctuary

'Rock of Ages cleft for me'—the saxifrage survives in a tiny crevice

He refused to part with anything. One day, the king asked him for a gem to decorate the temple.

The miser shook his head.

Nothing! He would give nothing.

Then a day came when his only daughter fell critically ill. As she gasped for breath, he realised that he would be much better off if he had given his riches to someone who could save the young girl. Desperately, he hurried off in that dark moonless night, to dig out the precious gems from a corner of his terraced-fields. In the dark, he stumbled, fell and died.

No one seems to know what happened to the daughter, but those glittering gems lay buried for many years afterwards, till one day, out sprouted from the earth a cluster of flowers, flecked with the colour of the gems that bore them.

Thus was born the *feinkamal*!

The dazzling Saint John's wort is reputed to banish all evil. Many tales are trapped around its yellow blossoms: if you're slightly touched, drink the red sap oozing from its leaves; if a wound does not heal, try the juice; and if your hair has run away, rise early, rub the dew off the petals on that bald pate and hair will sprout again or so the story goes.

Of course there is the blue Himalayan poppy, elusive, like a quick puff of smoke. Blue, deeper than any you've ever seen. Nature's favourite colour, trapped in crannies, catching the rays of the rising sun.

What is it then we look for in flowers? Is it the knowledge that flowers in their beauty perish? Yet their lovely freshness lingers in memory as the seasons melt into each other. They will be back again to cherish another day.

We all know that flowers may not fill a life. Perhaps they can only fill corners, which might otherwise be taken by cobwebs. At times, the dainty flowers, those that barely rise out of the ground, preferring to lie low and afraid to open their eyes, are the ones to stop and look at. Give a wide berth to the domineering ones—even the herdsmen's buffaloes grazing in the high-altitude meadows skirt around them.

As the rains end, it's time to rejoice. You'll catch the convolvulus sprouting forth its trumpet flowers—sufficient guarantee the sun will always emerge victorious.

With a few things, I too am like that old miser; guilty of hanging on to objects you would safely label 'sentimental'. What else would you call an old bookmark?

Left: Seeds of the wild ginger catch fire in autumn

Right: Sorrel comes in handy for shining brassware

A faded flower?

Or a jaded ribbon?

From that magical journey in school, I still possess an enchanted flower. Or does it possess me? I leave the debate open. For no rhyme or reason, I still keep it tucked away in an early copy of *Alice in Wonderland*. In that thunder lily, as flat as tissue, brittle to the touch are trapped warm memories of those days of wine and roses.

Even today, I do not have the heart to disturb this pale ghost of the flower. Was it given on a birthday? Or in just a passing moment?

I shall never know.

Many years later, I climbed the hills again. The trees looked dishevelled, covered in dust.

I wasn't there looking for those golden emperors—the *phyunlis*. They must have been asleep anyway. I took my fair companion to the old lyre tree, to show off my skill at carving its soft bark.

Puppy love didn't help and the memory gives faint outlines of that day.

A poignant moment, never to be forgotten, is as real to me today as if it were just yesterday, for first love is a tune without words, a plant without roots, and in the years ahead, only the sweet fragrance of bruised petals lingers. We came down the forest with the pines separating us.

Mr Garlah was not amused. 'You'll never make

Left: Cobra lily

Right: The gaudy seeds of the cobra lily belie the alkaloids they carry

a botanist my boy!' he pronounced.

How right he proved to be! I make no claims to knowing all the botanical names of the blooms, but I don't let that ever come between me and the miracle of wild flowers.

What happened to my fair lady, you fondly wonder. We met many years later, almost as strangers with a faint memory of a walk through a forest. She had a child with her, a little daughter with impish eyes, in which, I prefer to believe, lurked memories of the good days.

Last spring, I struggled up the fateful hill, a stranger lost in the chaos of an unkempt place. I'd promised a friend, a botanist of the fanatical variety (who would not rest till he'd conducted a frenetic post-mortem) to help find the legendary flowers. But I'd lost the eyes of childhood. I'd forgotten the charmed woods with fairies, goblins and elves in every nook and cranny. A long time passed before the genie of the glades relented. Had he forgiven me for the impetuous theft of long ago?

Perhaps not, for suddenly, under a thorny *kingora* bush, I saw a golden shaft nodding in the breeze and before I could as much as breathe, our keen botanist swooped hawk-like and uprooted the plant, flower, roots and all.

Decades later I found myself at the same crossroad again. The air seemed thick with betrayal.

I knew I had failed one more time. ●

Other Denizens of Garhwal

Morning breaks gently on the deodars—the tree of the gods

If it were possible to look upon our mountains as one huge pyramid, then most of the wildlife would be concentrated around the base, where the commonest creature is man. And he's done a fair bit to eliminate all the other species. He is in direct competition with the other denizens for more space.

Man is the new-age plague!

As the forests recede, where do the animals go?

Down into the fields they go to feed off the crops or the livestock!

In the foothills, among the oak, rhododendron and deodar forests you will often see troops of boisterous langurs feeding off the wild fruits or flower buds. What falls to the ground is snapped up by the barking deer and the round-horned ghoral.

Why do they hang around together?

As frightened as a langur or *Goni-daar* is a term of derision used by the mountain people to describe abject fear for it is said that the black-faced baboons climb to perches atop the tall limbs of these gossipy trees—way out of the reach of the other denizens of the forest.

And, at dusk, it is told in tales at twilight that the prowling panther makes his way home. He's hungry after a bad day at hunting. He stops a moment under the pines and soughs. As if on order, a scared baboon loses his grip and comes crashing down on to the forest floor. Dinner is served and the panther licks his lips as he saunters back home!

But the sloth bear, black and brown, prefer the upper ranges, along the edges of higher settlements which they raid for maize, pumpkins and squashes. When the

The mountains provide sustenance not only to its people but also animals

©Ambika Singh

crop is ready, he turns glutton to build up lard for his wintery hibernation. The amount of corn a bear will eat in one night, added to that which it tramples, makes quite a difference to a poor man's crop. So brazen-faced a robber is he that he'll think nothing of sitting down next to a hut feeding his fill; small wonder then that drums are beaten and torches lit to interrupt the rascal's feast. His eyesight is weak, but nature compensates him with a keen sense of smell. In a favourable wind, a Bruin can smell a quarry a quarter of a mile away even though he prefers the tender shoots of wheat and barley. The forest department would have us believe that there are nearly 2,000 bears in the state. It is the black bear which poses a threat to people living in the remote districts where they are known to enter homes; destroy property, and ruin cereals, wheat, rice and millet; and attack humans.

Of one such encounter, I was told: 'He was a very large male bearing the scars of three bullet wounds. Just the sight of his broad white chevron spread across his chest would scare the wits out of anyone. He cared for neither man nor dogs and went down fighting bravely.'

Fattened horses grazing in the meadows in the afternoon sun

Occasionally, women who go out in search of fuel and fodder are mauled by the black bear. 'It charged on all fours at a gallop,' a survivor tells me, adding: 'Like a great dog, its mouth wide open and making a loud angry grunt at every stride.' She lived to tell the tale by the simple expedient of climbing up a tree. Kipling once wrote:

When the Himalayan peasant meets the he-bear in his pride
He shouts to scare the monster, who will often turn aside.
But the she-bear thus accosted rends the peasant tooth and nail.
For the female of the species is more deadly than the male.

Though the brown bear is short-sighted, it makes up for this with his keen sense of smell. Sadly sometimes it is trapped and tragically taught to do all kinds of tricks at village fairs.

And do not get taken in by the appellation 'sloth' bear, for laziness has nothing to do with it. You will see it in the lower regions, the Terai, around swamps and marshes looking for anything that moves: ants, beetles, grasshoppers, termites.

'You should see how clever he is,' said our guide, pointing to a ravaged termite mound. 'A slash of his powerful claw opens up the nest, he blows out the dust and sucks the larvae clean.'

Though the boldest of all carnivores, the *chitrola* or the yellow-throated pine marten, black, brown and yellow, about the size of a big polecat, looks a bit like a Siamese cat, but looks can often be deceptive so don't you get taken in by its cute looks. Mostly living in moist deciduous forests, they are always on the move; hunting in pairs, running on the ground with the agility of a squirrel among the trees or hiding in rocky outcrops. I know these dogged hunters well, they can bring down others far larger than themselves. Cruel hunters who can follow their prey for long hours, even days, sometimes far behind, sometimes close, mostly by scent until the quarry wearies.

Atkinson in the *Himalayan Gazetteer* wrote:

> Some dogs chased a pair and caught one whilst the other took refuge in a tree; although the owner of the dogs was standing by encouraging them to kill the one that had been caught, the other came down from the tree and vigorously attacking the dogs perished in defence of its companion.

Elsewhere reports come in of them going over hills and through valleys for *two days* in pursuit of a barking deer. Ruthless hunters these who will not give up till their quarry tires and sits down to await certain doom.

At the apex of the ecological pyramid is the tiger. You will find him among the lush grasses of the Terai up to the Lower Himalaya. In *Man Eaters of Kumaon,* Jim Corbett narrates tales of tracking down some of these felines gone amok—one had killed 434 people falling to the hunter's gun. 'It is only when tigers have been incapacitated through wounds or old age that, in order to live, they are compelled to take to a diet of human flesh,' he wrote, almost apologetically.

For a man who spent thirty-two years of his life tracking down and shooting rogue leopards and tigers, he was a true conservationist, insisting:

A barn owl helps keep the rodent population under control

Far right: Tryst on a dandelion is good news for the meadows

> Those who have never seen a leopard under favourable conditions in his natural surroundings can have no conception of the grace of movement and beauty of colouring of this most graceful of animals. To class such

© Varun Shukla

an animal as vermin, as is done in some parts of India, is a crime which only those could perpetrate whose knowledge is limited to the miserable, underfed and mangy specimens seen in captivity.

Once upon a time, the Terai forests teemed with a plenitude of swamp deer, spotted deer and the sambhar. With the 'taming' of the Terai, which simply put just meant the death of the forests, the tigers where bereft of a prey base thus being reluctantly pushed into sanctuaries.

Often in the upper reaches of Garhwal, you shall come across the barking deer. It stands statue-still, senses straining, alert to the mere snapping of a twig. Its constant bark resonates through the valleys as it rarely leaves the relative safety of the slopes where it can hop from one promontory to the other. Of course, the famed musk deer too has been poached for its perfume-bearing pods.

Often, especially in the fall, the crack of butting ghorals resonates in the air. Using their spectacular horns as weapons, tilting like gladiators of yore, they charge at each other in rut. Both hold their ground, momentarily dazed. Don't for a moment believe that peace has come. Peace is far away—they are sizing up each other for another final joust.

Unfortunately, none of the glory washes off on the humble *runda*. They are also known as the pica or the mouse-hare—the last is misleading, for the diminutive denizen is neither mouse nor hare. Content living in the upper reaches, protected by a silky pelt, it overcomes bad eyesight by squeaking around the boulder-strewn landscape using echo-location to make its way home.

Sometimes in spring, on a dark moonlit night, I hear the familiar cry once again. The honking of a skein of wild geese as they wing their way across the mountains and beyond to truly go where no man has gone before. They continue to defy boundaries that mortals draw.

©Varun Shukla

A paradise flycatcher rests a moment in its search for food

Up until the turn of the nineteenth century, it was a commonly held belief that no bird could possibly fly across the barrier of the mighty Himalaya. True, they could skirt the riverine valleys, but nothing could go over the greatest barrier on the face of the earth. Mountaineering was to moderate this view.

As expedition after expedition reported in unison, birds could be seen in the day and heard at night crossing peaks that man had yet to climb. Explorer Sven Hedin saw ducks at the source of the Indus in Tibet and Eric Shipton found frozen ducks in the Karakorams. Triggered by an invisible biological clock they set off on journeys that take them beyond the ranges.

Our avian untouchables—hunters of carrion—lay claim to the highest realms. For what place could there be? In these frozen zones, death is the companion of despair where only the fittest survive. The weak and infirm perish to provide a ready larder for the birds circling above. The shadow that races across the ground is a griffon vulture checking out his domain. And he is never in a hurry. Wafted by the eddies of the breeze, he glides effortlessly on a ten-foot wing span, catching the thermals, covering tremendous distances in the search for carrion.

Then there's the lammergeyer—our bearded vulture—always seen in silhouette against the sun or the face of the mountains as it reaches incredible speeds of up to 80 miles an hour, skimming the contours with its eagle eyes scanning the earth below for a skeleton picked

© Varun Shukla

Powerful and intimidating, a cobra protects its territory

clean by the griffon vultures. Then, diving down, it will pick up large bones to fly back up into the air and let them go to shatter on the rock down below.

As I climb up the narrow trail, a swooshing sound makes me duck! Large formation of lammergeyers zooms by as if to announce my arrival to that world of peace and solitude.

This I know, the bird continues to thrive in the Garhwal-Kumaon Himalaya though it is almost extinct in its European homeland. Even a casual traveller will always catch it gliding along the eddies of the breeze. May they continue to prosper!

Along the ridges and low down in the valleys one hears the bamboo partridge sending forth his challenge in his exultant, though somewhat chaffing notes, as if defying the imaginary hunter to pursue him in his inaccessible home. Aware of his security, he ceases not his war song for the traveller. Nature has provided him with plumage that is in perfect harmony with his surroundings and it is indeed difficult for even the keenest bird-watcher to detect him in his home if he only sits tight!

Of all the birds in the high altitudes, my favourite is the chough. It looks like a crow but minus the greed. It is, I am convinced, an aesthete. This accomplished acrobat turns the Himalaya into an amphitheatre of pure delight as it flies to incredible heights, suddenly folds its dark wings and plunges thousands of feet to the valley floor like a rock, pulling out reluctantly just before it would be smashed on the ground down below.

And then to do it again and again.

What else is it but 'Art for Art's sake'?

Sir Edmund Hillary wrote of one persistent member of the family who insisted on accompanying him as he climbed from the last camp to 28,000 feet.

Not to be forgotten in a hurry are the smaller birds who do their bit in alpine pastures keeping a check on the insects hiding among the grassy slopes. I remember this pesky Simla tit, the size of a sparrow, which would start its breakfast of moths who had flown in from the forest to the light outside our home last night.

With the march of winter, the mountains are touched with a mantle of snow and an exodus of birds begins. Feathered flocks descend to the foothills, joining the hordes down below in forays for food and shelter. A miracle of adaptation is underway.

A red-bottomed pied woodpecker's breakfast of ripening walnuts

Mother Nature always takes care of her own. Nowhere is this truer than in the case of the blood pheasant you will meet at up to 15,000 feet. The male is a gaily coloured 'game bird' named after its distinctive stripes. However, the female does not have these bright colours as she must incubate the eggs in her perch on the cliff face. So she takes her colouring from the surrounding rocks, a dull, tedious brown.

The ornithologist's favourite is the one that got away: the elusive mountain quail, the *Ophrysia superciliosa.* The last live specimen was collected in 1876 from the area around Mussoorie; except for that, little is known of the bird. Early collectors tell us that the birds lived in groups of five or six, refusing to move out of the grass unless they were almost trampled upon.

Have we trampled it to extinction?

Its habitat was from Jharipani (home to the exiled Ranas of Nepal) through to Benog and Bhadraj at 7,000 feet. Little of the area remains as it must have been in the nineteenth century. First they *discovered* what everybody knew: the place was rich in limestone. Then the quarries began. You can still see the ugly scars.

In their wake came the carpetbaggers, the developers, and nothing was to ever be the same again. Mountains of concrete were poured to build dream homes.

For posterity, we have ten specimens of the mountain quail: five in the British Museum and the rest in America.

Yet, not all birds are simpletons like the mountain quail. The naughtiest of them all is the honeyguide of Nepal who takes after its African cousins in utter audacity.

How did it get its name?

It specialises in knowing the location of all the beehives in the forest. Be it a sharp rock face, a bee-nesting cliff or a hollow tree, the bird is willing to act as a willing guide to lead the honey-hunters. By a series of ingenious giveaways it takes the hunter, man or bear, to the hive. All this effort is richly rewarded with a share of the spoils: honey, larvae and wax after the honey has been stolen!

If you think this game of deception and betrayal was bad enough, you have another thing coming. The male honeyguide has been reported to take

The beech marten or the stone marten lives on a diet of rodents and birds

home bits of honeycomb to his personal territory throughout the year. Come breeding season and he mates with *all* the females whose sweet-tooth attracts them to his honeyed home.

We know that necessity is the mother of invention. But in the inscrutable ways of the honeyguide, an exception could be added: 'It is the smartest and not always the fittest who inherit the planet!'

After turning in at night, when all around was silent and still, I heard the eerie sounds of a weird rustling of wings, as if the restless spirits of the haunted mountain were flitting through the air. But the fear passed, for I soon discovered these came from several nightjars that were flying to and fro close over a surveyor's camp, probably disturbed by the moonshine on the white tents.

The nightjar, or goatsucker, reminds me of a little fable the hill people have about a small bird of the nightjar kind, which is rarely seen, although its 'too too' melancholy pair of notes can be heard at short intervals all night long among the oaks and rhododendrons.

The legend had it that once upon a time the birds of the wild had a mela of their own to which all the birds went. But this poor fellow, thinking his own plumage was not grand enough for the occasion, begged a bright-coloured feather from each of his more brightly dressed companions and went to the fair decked out in borrowed plumes. The fair over, the lenders demanded their feathers, but the new wearer, pleased with his new look, refused to return them.

Upon this, the others snatched for their feathers, and in the rough-and-tumble scuffle, the poor borrower was stripped, not only of them, but of most of his own too!

So this modest bird has ever since been lamenting its fate, striving to hide its nakedness, which, the hill folk say, accounts for the mournful notes and its being seen so seldom.

Today, like on other occasions too, I set off to find the bird by trying to follow it up when it starts off on its sad notes. Strange, but once again I fail to find it.

Easy to find are the chattering magpies (the blue and white with yellow beak and long waving tail, called *'sanjara'* in the hills) flying noisily among the fruit trees; or sometimes a golden oriole darts across the forest like a shooting star. Or you might chance upon a pair of partridges feeding in the fields; the cock bird strutting on a rock puffing out his chest, bowing and scraping and turning around as he sings a torrent of affection to his mate feeding nearby.

Not all is quiet in the Himalaya. Round a tree-covered spur, the koklass pheasant is heard. It is a strange noise, and sounds as if it were only half-finished, like that of a young cockerel learning to crow.

Around me, the air is still. No breeze stirs the leaves of the brooding trees. From high above comes the yelping of a dog. But I know it cannot be a dog, for the simple reason dogs cannot fly. It is the shrill cry of a pair of Himalayan golden eagles, those majestic birds, monarchs of the sky, scanning the earth below. Taking off from inaccessible eyries, they sound like a plane leaving the ground; given their longevity, these homes pass from one generation to another forever.

A musk deer—much hunted for its fragrant pods

Haunting the wild country, snapping up incautious animals at will, a sight that struck terror in the hearts of the early explorers who found the locals referred to them as *daags* or witches. Preferring to hunt in pairs, one drives and harries, the other swoops down with the deadly accuracy of a compressed air pistol! Hunting like falcons, dropping with tremendous speed, striking with its hind claws it rips open its prey at a bare touch. And the sparsely scrubbed mountainside teems with chokers, stopcocks and monal pheasants. ●

Great Spirits of the Himalaya

The dry meadows of Kushkalyani

A superstition, or a tale, is at home in a place, like a plant it draws vitality from a certain environment, and will not flourish anywhere else. For example, take the Garhwal hills, lying along the rivers of the Yamuna and the Ghagra, which is an ideal setting for some picturesque folklore.

Pastures here are poor, and the hill folk, who keep large herds of cattle, live in little slate-roofed or thatched hamlets, wide-sundered from one another. Their lives are hard and can, sometimes, be very lonely. Their hopes are sown with the corn, in stony soil; every passing breeze fans their fears. Loneliness works on the imagination and endows the little-known and the remote with immense importance. And if the forests around them contain friends, they also give shelter to many foes.

From earliest times men have feared the owl. Some have considered it unlucky, others have taken its presence as an omen. Often it has provided many ingredients for the witches' cauldron, and its heart was considered to be the vehicle of many potent charms. The eagle owl, largest of the family, is not the most attractive: his life is a long nightmare of deadly encounters and long periods of unwinking watchfulness. His eyes blaze with cunning, and a certain cruel wisdom.

Both the Garhwali and Kumaoni alike dread its eerie call! All over these mountains, you often are told: 'This bird is Death's emissary, who warns the fated of their end. He will call above that man's roof, or flap his wings against the door. Death is then announced, whether it comes in a day or a week, it doesn't matter!'

Religious rituals form an intrinsic part of the lifestyle of the hill folk

The life of the wild invades even the fireside, and many tales are told of the wilfulness and cunning of wild creatures. The little story that follows enshrines a belief widely held in these parts of the Himalaya that a male bear will never attack a woman—except under very special circumstances.

Once upon a time, three pretty girls were sent out by their parents to collect fodder. Hunting about for the best, they at last found themselves on

© TS Chauhan

a steep and precipitous slope which was far from their village, but on which the grass grew lush and plentiful. The place was very lonely, and, sure of privacy, they set to work with merry abandon. By twilight they had collected enough to carry home.

Somewhat weary after the unaccustomed labour they sat down to rest, unmindful of the passing of time. Just then a bear, who was setting out on his nocturnal search for acorns, happened to come that way, attracted, no doubt, by the girls' voices. Finding them all very attractive, he began to woo them very ardently, or so the story goes.

The first maiden briefly disdained his addresses, whereupon, enraged, he tore her limb from limb and flung her remains over a neighbouring precipice.

The second girl, likewise stubborn, suffered a similar fate. But the third, who was exceedingly cunning, lured the bear to the very edge of the cliff. She manoeuvred him to come between herself and the fall; then quickly exerting all her strength, she

Venerated by millions, a combination of spiritual and physical marvels unequalled in the world

pushed him suddenly, so that he plunged backwards over the brink and was killed on the rocks far below!

Another correspondent reports this story from the hills in 1910:

> It would appear that Master Bruin was enamoured of a certain young woman in a village, and he had been known to make frequent nocturnal visits to her home, but without success. Bruin however came down the hill one evening earlier than usual, and finding the young damsel by herself in a field, made a bold dash and, amid shouts of the villagers, carried her off in triumph to his craggy home. Was this elopement, kidnapping or abduction? If only it was cognizable, the police and the legal profession might have made a harvest out of it.
>
> As the cave was inaccessible the men were helpless; they despaired of the life of the young woman but cherished ideas of bitter revenge. Deep plans were laid to this end. It was not long before Bruin fell into the trap, and when he came down for his afternoon feed of cucumbers, corn and *mandua*, of which he is said to be fond, his retreat was cut off. He made a good fight for liberty but was overpowered and fell at the hands of his enemies.

Whatever happened to the young woman, you might wonder. The villagers climbed down a cliff over-hanging the cave in which the bear was known to have lived. One of the men, bolder than the rest, descended by means of a long rope secured to a rock, and when he arrived opposite the cave, to his great surprise, he found the woman alive.

How do I get her out of here, he wondered. It was impossible for her to climb up the way the man had descended, so more help and more rope had to be procured and sent down to the cave. The woman was finally let down by means of a basket, and all returned to their homes amidst great rejoicings.

When monsoon mists shroud these hills and lodge mystery in every nook and glen, it is the season for *momiai,* and time for a ghostly band of man-hunters to commence their activities. *Momiai* is an old superstition about a magic unguent, which confers invulnerability against all weapons, and is unrivalled for the quick healing of wounds. It's extracted from the human cranium! I've heard stories of these mountain legions as a child but let me tell you how I heard it from Nathuram, the headman of my village:

> There is a tribe of men whose whole business it is to collect *momiai.* They are a brutal and unscrupulous lot, who frequent lonely roads on the lookout for solitary travellers. They carry long staves, in the ends of which are secreted certain essences which, if a man smells them, immediately deprives him of his rightful senses. If perchance a traveller comes that way, they make up to him, and by pure trickery, beguile him into smelling the rod. Instantly, his senses forsake him, and then the evil ones take

© TS Chauhan

Pilgrims at Madhmaheswar, one of the Panch Kedars

> him away into the jungle where their accomplices await their arrival. The victim is bound and strung, with his head hanging over a cauldron. Beneath the cauldron a big fire is lit. They knock a hole in the victim's head; the *momiai* trickles out, drop by drop, and collects in the vessel below. Afterwards the body of the man is buried, and all traces of the deed are carefully effaced, so that thereafter never a trace of the traveller may be found.

The only *beings* whose reputation approaches anywhere near that of the *momiai* hunters are the ghosts or spirits, for Himalayan ghosts have a reputation for originality and live up to it. The *churail*, or *churain* as it is sometimes called, adopts some queer practices in these parts.

Kharsali, home to the pundits of Yamnotri

The *churail* may never be seen, but it is reputedly a common experience for a man to be accosted and spoken to by it. It takes great delight in pelting stones after him as he runs away downhill. Or it may attack him by hurling him on his back, and then mauling him as a wild cat would! *Churails* are supposedly the spirits of women who died in childbirth, or those who did not receive proper funeral rites.

Or take the chilling tales of *masan, pret, khabes* and *bhuts,* told at twilight in the courtyards of the mountain villages. It is said that all ghosts are the souls of those who died a violent death, or were denied due funeral rites. Take the *ranbhuts* or the spirits of valiant warriors who found martyrdom in battle, whose spirits return to possess fellow clansmen at the time of festivals. To drive them away, you'll have to know *rakholis*—magic incantations known only to believers!

Then there are the playful *acharis* or fairies, better known for carrying away handsome warriors to their elfin caves.

For sheer effect, there are no spirits to vie with the *pichachas,* which have become the playthings of Destiny. It is said that by day they may sometimes be heard bewailing their unhappy lot as they stray over the hills on their ceaseless wanderings.

By night they are visible as torches of ethereal fire, which wheel and shift with the spirits' movements. It is at night that they climb to the summits, and may then be seen, like a fallen galaxy, spangling some desolate mountaintop.

Occasionally, we are to believe, they have been approached, from a respectful distance, by certain

braves and their 'aura' examined and later described: 'A sheaf of crimson flames within a mist of light.'

Mountains have always beckoned to the dwellers on the plains, though it still remains impossible to capture its charm. I think the *pichachas* come very near to revealing it: they might be the spirits of the place, for mountains have many moods.

But the moods of those who climb those dizzying heights are filled with tales of ghosts. Climbing a peak in Lahoul, Robin Hamer writes:

> An interesting and intriguing curiosity occurred during the time we were in the mountains. A mountain dog attached itself to the expedition which we fed and allowed to sleep in the tent. The dog eventually went as high as the first icefall at 17,000 ft. Whilst on the KR glacier system Lai Chand clearly heard a woman's voice calling to him. Lizzie, the only woman, was a kilometre away sat with the others and had said nothing. At the same time the hair on our placid dog's back went up and she ran around barking. There was no one else in the area. Secondly, on the night of the 13 September while we were away the dog went crazy again, hair standing up as it rushed into Lizzie's tent barking. All three people, lying in their tents at base camp, heard footsteps on the moraine walking around the camp and off towards the glacier. No one was there or could have been there. The porters say the spirit of an English woman stays in that region of the mountains.

The allusion perhaps is to Miss Hilda Richmond who came out with an expedition in 1939. The group leader wrote:

> The morning of 14th September brought us the finest weather ... At lunchtime, Miss Richmond failed to appear. She had often been late when collecting plants. A search party found Miss Richmond dead in a steep gully not far from the Base Camp. She had meant to have a wash—she had a towel with her—and had therefore followed the course of the stream upward into the steep rocks till she found a pool of clear water. There she was hit on the head by a falling stone and was killed instantly.

A rough memorial of stone marks the grave. Her companions named the peak she had climbed, Richmond Peak. •

Dharali: A Place for All Reasons

Tented colony at Dharali

This summer if you want to get away from the heat and dust to cooler climes, make sure to choose lesser-known places in the hills. This is so because in the crowded hill stations you'll find it hard, at times, to even get water to quench your thirst. Forget those hoardings with attractions like waterbeds thrown in! Some places you'll be lucky to get enough water to brush your teeth! Honestly, last season's tourists had to look around for soda for reasons other than whisky.

As for the other hill resorts in the north, the visitor has to be in good jogging practice. Last time traffic jams had cars stranded six kilometres away from the glitter of the hills. Safer getaways are the yet undiscovered places of the Garhwal region, such as Dharali, Chopta, Duggalbetta, Chamba and Chandrashila.

If you prefer to get away from it all—without hauling a mountain of equipment—then Dharali is a place for all reasons. How many of us have wished to camp out in a comfortable tent along the river, gazing at the stars, with not a worry in the world! Of course as you look at the amphitheatre of the gods, you'll get some inkling of why they say 'Time is the child of Eternity'.

On the day I was there, there was not a soul around. An old weathered parchment caught in a *chimul* bush, as the rhododendron is called here, struggled with the wind to set itself free. A sudden gust and it was off. Trapped by the breeze it flew thousands of feet away till it was lost to sight.

I came down the face of the mountain spirit refreshed and whole again.

Duggalbetta stands like an orchid in Chamoli District

There are no hassles getting there either. I was to discover all this and more along the banks of the gentle river, the Bhagirathi, just twenty kilometres before Gangotri. Indeed, still a place in the world untouched by the machinations of man.

At a tented colony, you'll discover all the creature comforts you could possibly need and more. After a day of undisturbed rest, you'll awaken just before dusk in a scene straight out of the Arabian Nights—a blazing log fire, strictly of driftwood carried by the river, on the tranquil sands of the river. And you won't have to pay with an arm and a leg either: there are dormitories for students or others on a shoestring budget or a fully carpeted tent at 500 rupees a night for sheer luxury.

What will you do there? All those things you've dreamt of and never got down to doing. Relax awhile, with the soft turf as a couch, a gnarled root as a good pillow, and a bubbling stream singing a soothing lullaby. Slowly but surely your thoughts drift over the hills to the plains far away, which you left but a few days ago, and as you take in gulps of the diamond air, it'll all seem to fade away as if it were a world well-forgotten. Indeed there shall be time to see the flowers at your feet: kingcups by the water—forcing their way through the slush of melting snow; and add to this the promise of many more yet to come.

Upstream, at a point where three mountain torrents merge into each other, is Harsil, which was once home to Raja Wilson, who married a local young woman and settled down in Wilson Hut. No hut this, but a magnificent bungalow. Yes it was! In an act of monumental neglect, it caught fire a winter's night and one cannot put out a fire with snow! Of course, I'm told an enquiry is afoot, and we all know what that means—nothing! Given time we compromise with anything. I remember this harmonious blend of stone and wood, permanent reminder of the freebooter, F.E. Wilson, from the 1850s. Immense tracts of blue pines, pencil cedars and deodars attracted his attention. Leasing these forests from the Raja of Tehri in 1859, undeterred by the lack of roads, he floated timber down the Ganga to be used as sleepers for the railways. Naturally, very soon, he had made a huge fortune.

The old forest rest houses at Dharasu, Bhatwari and Harsil were his staging posts along the narrow trail that snaked its way from one village to the other. As if this were not enough, he introduced the apple into this area, and if you are offered a large red apple you can be sure you have stumbled upon a Wilson apple.

Bridge building was another of Wilson's interests. One of these was meant to ease travel between Harsil and the holy shrine at Gangotri. The most famous of these was a 350-foot suspension bridge over the Jadh Ganga at the stupendous gorge of Bhaironghati—over 1,200 feet off the valley floor. This shaky contraption was at first a source of great terror to the locals, and none would venture across. To reassure the hill folk, he mounted his grey stallion and galloped to and fro across the planks. The original bridge has succumbed to the sandpapering of Time but

Mussoorie's Charleville Hotel was called Charlie-Billy Hotel

people will tell you that the hoof beats of his horse can still be heard on full moon nights.

Wilson's life is a fit subject for a romance. His legend lives on. Though no attempts have been made to glorify him, the residents still speak of him in awe and admiration, almost as if he had just gone by yesterday. Some men give their spirit to a place and become a part of its love and legend.

Should you feel like travelling further upstream, you will arrive at Gangotri, the source of the mighty Ganga. But do make sure you return to the splendid solitude of your tent at Dharali, for at Gangotri there's little left to commend the place. The exhausts of numberless buses create a pall of smoke and drown out the pleasures of old.

Sometimes I'm left wondering how much longer do we have before these little out-of-the-way places get overrun and lose it all.

Just six kilometres away is Chopta, where the Garhwal Mandal Vikas Nigam chose a prized spot to set up a bungalow. It used to be clean, inexpensive and, best of all, uncrowded. But I've heard there is a rough patch with locals protesting about the attempts being made to encroach on more land. For the time being it's all in the courts. Above Chopta, the trees vanish most abruptly, as if some old surveyor had drawn an invisible line and forbidden the trees to take root.

Beyond it all lies windswept Tungnath. Hire a pony to get there if the climb is not really your cup of tea. This is the highest shrine in the inner Himalaya.

Don't forget to tarry awhile as you come down the great mountains. Surrender yourself to the quaint charms of Chopta. Watch the fading light glint off the rocks that lie along the path. Yes! You could call it a ladder to heaven.

Wayside shrine bear scars of the wars of the past centuries

For the more daring, there is the climb to Chandrashila, the highest peak in the inner Himalaya, a bleak, rock-strewn place, perched atop a crag. On its rocky peak you'll discover the borders where religions meet and mingle. For centuries, the inhabitants of the high mountains have come here to pay oblations to the dead and leave behind the horoscopes of those who've gone before us. You'll find little piles of rocks, *pitra kudha*, I'm told, so much like the chortens of the Buddhists.

And if you look down, far, far below along the distant road you'll see the villages of Garhwal. Simple structures of mud, earth, slates, and weathered wood, bunched together against the slopes as if for comfort. The faint shadow of an invisible line plays through the speckled shadows of a coniferous forest—it is the only trace of the road travelled on just a few hours ago. ●

A Return To Uttarkashi

Remote villages house only the old, infirm, women and children

The ancients built Barahaat as a *'barra-haat'*—a big market at the base of a lofty mountain, around a bend on that river of faith, the solemn Bhagirathi.

Oh! How well I know, the town does not reveal its antiquity, at least not all too easily, preferring instead to keep its secret hidden so much like the lines on the palm of one's hand, those infinite cracks, finer than the gossamer threads of a spider's web glistening with dewdrops at dawn.

Those tales are kept only for the initiated, those who can tread very softly along a path long vanished, with the railing twisted, the telephone poles tilted, bridges mangled and many memories gouged into each bit of man's efforts to make them look like a patchwork quilt put out in the sun.

'Sometimes, the ground swells and shrugs,' says Murari Singh, an old-time vegetable vendor near the bus stand, adding, 'Of course, the town trembles, windows chatter, dogs bark and the town awakens, shuddering.' The moment passes, shaking off the dust, Uttarkashi begins another day. Life goes on. Like the mythical phoenix, the town rises out of the ashes of the past, dusts itself to begin life anew.

Always a place of importance down the ages, it was here that all the pilgrims' trails converged at the town square: Gangotri just seven days away, Yamnotri, seven, Srinagar en route to Badrinath, six, and Kedarnath, twelve.

Even today, on a dark night, if you listen carefully over the road of the river and if you can ignore the thumping of your heart, you too will hear the tinkling of the bells. Those

Uncluttered Kedarnath Temple in the 1970s

Where every single rock appears to be God's own image

caravans of the past, when the sturdy Bhotias came down the treacherous passes with asafoetida, *jakhya*, *choru* and saddle bags bulging with salt, borax and onions.

Shakabpa, the Tibetan historian tells us: 'Every Tibetan, be he a trader, a monk, an official, a soldier or a pilgrim, travelled by horse, mule or foot. Luggage was carried by horse, yak, mule, ox, donkey or sheep.'

In the western parts of Tibet, sheep were the commonest pack animal, each carrying two ten-pound loads of salt. Each trader had about a hundred sheep and about a dozen traders moved together. The load was never removed from the sheep's back for several weeks. Often, at the end of the long journey when the load was finally removed, skin came away with the load. At the border posts, the sheep too were sold off with the salt.

From Barahaat, they took away wool, cotton, silk, kerosene, glass, iron, copper, rice, fruit and medicinal herbs.

However, this border trade ended as the giants of war shrugged to the north. For as early as 1948, when few foresaw the unfolding of events, we are told:

> The Tibetans were greatly disturbed by many baleful portents: A gilded dragon that decorated the pagoda roofs of Jo-Kang – the Cathedral of Lhasa – was seen to drip water from its mouth in dry weather; in the nights, a great comet blazed in the sky; monstrous births were reported and finally the canopy of an ancient stone pillar at the foot of the Potala fell inexplicably one night.

Soon, the abode of the snow, the lost horizon, was to be swept away by an avalanche of man's making. And so the trading-fairs at Uttarkashi came to a tragic end.

Wishes are fulfilled at the Udak-kund at Kedarnath

Long before these turbulent times, in AD1634, the intrepid traveller, Hiuen Tsang came through here on his way to Haridwar. His memoirs make interesting reading as he found the kingdom of Brahmapura 4000 li or 666 miles in circuit, surrounded on all sides by mountains. The capital, small, but the inhabitants, many and prosperous. He writes:

> They are followers of both the Buddhist and Brahminical faiths. There are five monasteries within which reside a few monks and there are around a dozen temples.
>
> To the north is Sou-fa-la-nakin-ta-lo or Suvarnagotra where gold of a superior quality is obtained. The men occupy themselves with war and husbandry. The soil is fertile and is favourable to the growth of a poor kind of barley, and the people rear many sheep and ponies. The climate is icy cold and the inhabitants are abrupt and turbulent in their manners.

Barahaat, once the seat of an old dynasty, still has many remains of temples and other buildings. The inscription on the trident of Aneka Malla dates back to the twelfth century, you can see it in the old temple wall. During the earthquake of 1803, Barahaat suffered much and all the buildings were completely buried. Two or three hundred perished.

It's cold outside; even the stars have an icy twinkle. A moon comes over the dark mountains, turning the Bhagirathi into a river of molten silver. The wind pants through the trees, making them dance in a mad frenzy outside my window. We are at the very epicentre of the last earthquake. Here, in this remote place, it all remains as real as I go through my old journal entries:

> *Village Didsari:* A seventy-year-old man sits on a slate tile courtyard for lunch. Before he eats, he makes seven neat little heaps around his plates as tears well up in his eyes. Each is for the seven sons crushed to death that autumnal night a year ago.
>
> *Village Jamak:* Eighty were extricated from the rubble of the reinforced concrete roofs. Pilfered cement from the nearby power project was so freely available, the entire village switched over to modern

Nandi's eternal wait for Lord Shiva outside Kedarnath Temple

material and paid a heavy price. The traditional mud-and-slate houses withstood the buckling, developed a few cracks but survived.

Uttarkashi: Badri Prasad Jasola, the sub-divisional magistrate, was chosen to oversee relief operations. To this day, he cannot get past the enormity of human suffering, 'Cremating innocents breaks the heart—almost brought me to the brink of renunciation.'

Bhatwari: Word trickles in that downstream, the diversion tunnel of the Tehri Dam is intact. 'What if the next quake is eight on the Richter?' exclaims Narain Prasad, a school teacher, adding: 'It could be ten times worse, wrenching the mountains like matchsticks.

In 1934, Eric Shipton and H.D.Tilman opened up exploration of the Garhwal Himalaya

Cyril Raphael remembers the countrywide response, especially the non-governmental organisations. 'It puts one's faith back in the essential goodness of the human race,' he tells me.

Seema Gaikwad, whose social service group took an early plunge into relief work, reminisces:

> We happened to be on the other side of Bhaldiyana bridge. Our immediate task was medical aid to the ·victims, removal of the dead and extricating belongings from the rubble before the snow set in. Thank heavens for the brave boys of the Indo-Tibetan Border Police and others—the damage was contained. The pressure is greater today. With the media circus gone, we have the living to look after—the widowed, the orphaned, the new-born and the old.

Athough the professors at the local college argue about everything, they are unanimous about one: the energy of the tectonic plates has not been fully released and the next quake could be something else. Consider this, when given the fact that our seismic knowledge is so limited that it was some time before Agora—a few kilometres away—and not Almora in faraway Kumaon, was finally confirmed as the epicentre!

After the event, if you can call it that, the only person who seemed to make some kind of sense is the self-effacing leader of the Chipko movement, Chandi Prasad Bhatt, who said: 'We can only move forward with our eyes fully open. The entire gamut of planning has to be rescheduled. Acute backwardness of the area existed long before the earthquake. This is not relief to the people—it's compensation for years of neglect.'

He couldn't possibly be more right! •

Where Rivers Run Deep

At Rudraprayag the Alaknanda meets the Mandakini

Let us go, you and I, away from all this to the mountains of Garhwal, where rivers run deep and legends spring from the land.

My old-time favourite, born in the monsoons, hangs in the air of Maletha on the road to the higher peaks beyond the ranges.

The night was uneasy. Sleep eluded him again. Madho Singh Bhandari, soldier and warrior, of some 400 years ago, had returned home to find the fields parched by yet another drought. In the recent past, he had worked ceaselessly on an aqueduct through the mountains to bring water from the Chandrabhaga River for the weather-plagued fields. But ill-luck continued to dog his venture.

And now the mountain spirits were wreaking havoc. In the monsoon, the bus creaks to a halt. The lush paddy crop bears eloquent testimony to this legend from the valley of the Alaknanda. The *hurkia's* drums tell of a tale of sacrifice at twilight. If you as much as dare sigh, you are bound to be ticked off. Any bystander will remind you: '*Ek singh rann koh!/Ek singh ban koh!/Ek singh Madho Singh!/Aur singh Kaiko?*' (A lion in the battle field, a lion in the forest, a lion in Madho Singh, are there other lions?)

Roopkund does not reveal her icy secrets except in snowmelt

With angry images of brimstone and fire, the spirits asked for his nine-year-old son, Gajai, before the entrapped waters of the river could debouch on the little hamlet.

Torn between need and love, Madho Singh paced through the night. What should he do? What could he do? The answer came at dawn. 'It is time the waters came. My time is up. Come father! Let us go,' calmly said the lad.

Who was braver? Gajai or Madho Singh? I dare not hazard a guess. But whenever the wind plays truant with the emerald fields it whistles: 'Both!'

The bus starts fitfully. We jump in on-the-run and are across the new bridge that skirts the old township of Kirtinagar. Historians tell us of sixty generations of the royal house of Garhwal who ruled over this area from AD 756. Each ruler preferred to build a new town.

In the seventeenth century, Shyam Shah ruled Garhwal. He was a liberal ruler, even allowing a Jesuit to build a house near his palace and practise his own beliefs. An impatient man, he ordered the disarming of some Nagas who insisted on taking their weapons with them after the Kumbh Mela on a yatra to Badrinath. On their refusal to comply, he asked his troops to expel them from his state. After his morning court, he would ride a caparisoned elephant to the home of his mistress and after wine, women

At Devprayag, the waters of the Bhagirathi River seem to halt as they mingle with the Alaknanda River

and song, the evening entertainment was scheduled to begin. One sultry monsoon day of July l631 he was out with his entourage boating on the swollen Alaknanda when his boat capsized and he drowned. It is said that at his cremation, sixty queens of the royal harem jumped into his pyre to commit sati.

Then a tale began to do the rounds, according to which his spirit would wander around the town in royal regalia. On one of these wanderings, he bumped into the son of one of his teachers, and the ghostly king gave him a bagful of gold coins and asked him not to tell a soul about it. But just to make sure, the ghost left him with a stutter so that he could never complete the tale.

Kirti Shah, at the turn of the nineteenth century, lent his name to the village of Biloli. A man of Spartan habits, he spent most of his time assembling searchlights or gazing at the stars. But not for long. At thirty, while raising the Garhwal Sappers, this gentle soul passed away.

Rudraprayag stands at the confluence of the Alaknanda and Mandakini rivers

Not all the kings were as gentle and his son Narendra Shah's rule was marked by callous neglect. Especially the barbaric treatment meted out to freedom fighters like the twenty-nine-year-old Sridev Suman who was thrown into jail and found martyrdom, after an eighty-four-day-long hunger-strike, on 25 July 1944 in Tehri.

Sometimes, I think the waters of the submontane rivers here have been kinder to the memory of the kings of Garhwal than public memory. With monotonous regularity, they have washed away all the bitterness of the past. The erstwhile capital of Srinagar today serves as the headquarters of the Garhwal University. It was here that the seventeenth-century painter and poet made exquisite miniatures. Where are his favourites, those *mandar* trees? Were they the ancestors of our magnolias? No one can tell.

Natural calamities of disastrous magnitude have visited the place over the ages. Gone too are the palaces of the rajas, with flash floods or earthquakes. In 1803, the earth moved beneath Garhwal, once again destroying homes, killing human beings and cattle. 'The town of Srinagar was nearly destroyed,' wrote Raper on a visit in 1808, 'not above one home in five was inhabited, the rest being heaps of ruins.' Much later, Batten observed: 'The Raja's palace was rendered inhabitable. Frequent shocks took place for several months. It is said that many streams had run dry, whilst new springs appeared in other places.'

Nestled in this wide open valley, surrounded by high mountains, this is the place where in 1805 the ancestors of the Garhwali soldiers (who have a tradition of gallantry in times of war) made their last but unsuccessful stand against the Gurkha invaders from the north.

Then again, in 1894 the Gohna Dam burst and swept away the town almost to the very last stone. This natural dam was born of a landslide in the valley of the Birahi Ganga, miles upstream, and as the edges of the dam crumbled, ten billion cubic feet of water gushed down the river, sweeping away every single bridge up to downstream Haridwar.

Srinagar rose again near the centre of a wide flat a mile away from the old site. Even today, as you walk along the riverbed you could see the remains of older temples. Sister Nivedita wrote: 'They are small, but marvelously perfect. The style must have persisted long in the Himalaya. There are examples of it, in a more developed and slender form, even here in Srinagar, as modern as 200 years but earliest examples must be very old, about 400 AD.'

In 1624 a Jesuit monk, Father Antonio de Andrade, went to the Garhwal court at Srinagar. He was the first European to enter Garhwal, having arrived in Goa in 1600. This Jesuit was on a journey to Tibet to bring back to the fold the lost Tibetan Christians. They were firm in the belief that Tibetan Buddhism was but a form of early Christianity and because of a lack of proper missionary guidance, they had strayed from the true path. Andrade and his companions, Father Manuel Marques and two Indian Christian servants, joined a group of pilgrims at Delhi, who were off on a pilgrimage to the shrines of Badri-Kedar.

Swami Manmathan, a social activist and reformer changed the face of Anjani Sain

At Haridwar, the Mughal frontier guards mistook them for runaways from the Mughal Empire whilst the Garhwal Guards felt they were spies who wanted to infiltrate the area. A few days were to go by before they could convince the authorities on both sides of their real mission.

On 11 April 1626, Andrade laid the foundation of a church at Chaprand in Tibet.

April of 1785 could not have been such a cruel month after all. For aboard the East Indiaman *Atlas* were two artists who would leave an indelible mark on the way we were one day to look back upon Garhwal. A thirty-six-year-old Thomas Daniell and his sixteen-year-old nephew William secured permission from the East India Company to undertake the long journey around the Cape of Good Hope to come to India.

Four years later, after traversing the long coastline of India, they were to go where no European of any consequence had ever been—the Garhwal Himalaya. In spring, they set off with an escort of four British officers and fifty sepoys and waited in Najimabad for permission, through the good offices of a local official, to be able to travel through the hills and into the unexplored territory to the north.

Under the eagle-eyed Captain Guthrie and Lieutenant Strumer, the group set off on foot to Kotdwara in the foothills; before them lay a four-day march along the river. This bit, easy, for the real

NGO representatives distributing relief after the last flash floods

climb into the hills lay on ahead. William in his diary notes with delight the familiar stinging nettle which he had not seen since setting out from home. Soon after, the conifers appeared and he knelt down to pick the yellow raspberries to add a touch of home to his pudding. 'We're all greatly disappointed,' he wrote, 'in not finding the hill men ready to march with us—on that account were obliged to halt another day. Gave the hill men some money in the morning which induced the others to come and offer their services.'

The infamous *jampans* or carrying chairs can be seen in their sketches, lying under the ample shade of a tree. You can see it on the engraving entitled *Coaduwar Gaut*: Kotdwara, at the door of the pass into the high mountains.

Jhawanu, we are told, was a small irregular place. The zamindar, or chief landowner of the neighbourhood, was lodged more 'sumptuously' than his inferiors. His mansion was tolerably better—built of stone, covered with slate, and consisted of two floors: the upper one would accommodate the chief and his family, the lower afforded shelter to his cattle.

They were not impressed by the zamindar and his ways. It was the villagers of whom they observed:

> Security is a principal source of happiness. The peaceful inhabitants of these hills not only enjoy a secure retreat from the perils of polished society, but a luxuriant vegetation supplies them with food,

© TS Chauhan

Over two hundred lakes alike Kakbhushandi Tal lie hidden in these mountains

> and also with gums and other articles of commerce, with which, by sale or barter, they procure from the distant plains such conveniences as their moderate system of life requires.

At a place called Naithana, on 25 April they reached a ridge from atop which they got their first glimpse of those 'veiled deities' to the north. The height of those titans was much more than they ever expected. William wrote:

> From Naithana ascended a very high mountain from which we had a glorious view of the Snowy ones, or rather regions. The height of them far exceeded any of our expectations – they disappeared soon after the sun had risen. On our march we saw many noble scenes – most of the mountains are cultivated from top to bottom. The Cuckoo is the only bird we have seen or heard for many days. Met with the pines again chiefly on the northern sides of the mountains – also daisies in great plenty, the dandelion, rushes, the butter flower, St. John's Wort and the honeysuckle is a strong woody shrub.

After this the trek resembled a game of snakes-and-ladders, up one ridge and down the other. But the magical 'hour of the cow-dust' defied the artists and they lamented:

> The visionary effect of the twilight. The beauty of the fireflies was still further out of the reach of imitative art: they illuminated every object, and diffused a magical radiance equally beautiful

> and surprising: it seemed in truth to be a land of romance, and the proper residence of those fanciful beings, the fairies and genie, that appear so often in Asiatic tales.

At last arriving above the vale of Srinagar, they pitched their tents to the south-west and took in the panorama of the town with the wide swath of the Alaknanda River flowing through it.

Three exciting days followed.

As they were the first Europeans in the area, the word of their arrival spread very fast and hordes of locals flocked to gaze at them. While at dusk, Raja Pradhyuman Shah and his younger brother, Prakaram Shah came by amidst much fanfare and trumpeting. He was presented with a watch and two pistols. But ill tidings were to reach their camp next morning. It was apparent that the raja was at war with the neighbouring king and it seemed that the invaders would be knocking at the gates of the town in a few hours.

Kholi-ku-Ganesh or the Lord Ganesha of the Threshold

With typical British phlegm, the Daniells set off to examine the rope bridge across the river. It was rocking and rolling with the crush of people fleeing with their belongings. On their return, William approved of the gifts brought by the raja's attendants: three superb birds, some musk and a yak's tail!

And then, the next day, the raja was back.

At first, it seemed that he had merely come to ask how the watch and pistols worked. Captain Guthrie obliged by giving them some gunpowder. They promptly pressed the trigger with disastrous results—a broken matchlock and a dislocated shoulder.

Meantime, the raja seemed most preoccupied. It was quite some time before he revealed the true purpose of his visit. Could their British escort help him against the invading enemy?

Prudence was the watchword and not wanting to get involved in a local fracas, it was decided to retreat from the town. They had been there only five days. What would have been the result if they had come in more peaceful times? But then it is one of those 'Ifs' of history!

As they climbed up the mountain, the smoke from the ransacked villages rose in the blue sky and they knew it was time to get back to the security of the Raj.

Not till 1796 would another European set foot in those mysterious mountains to the north of the Great Plains of northern India. And Thomas Hardwicke was no artist, he was a botanist! And thereby hangs another tale ...

Gangotri Temple built by Amar Singh Thapa and later renovated by the Maharaja of Jaipur

The founders of the Garhwal school of painting, Shyam Das and Har Das, father and son, came to the court of Raja Prithipat Shah (1625-1660) in Srinagar in May 1658 along with the refugee prince Suleman Shikoh, son of Aurangzeb's brother Dara. The Mughal prince wanted to join his father Dara in Lahore but wanting to avoid encounter with Aurangzeb's forces, he travelled from Allahabad to Nagina with seventeen courtiers and servants. They were to stay in Srinagar for one year and seven months but were betrayed by the crafty heir apparent Medini Shah in a contrived skirmish.

Shaym Das and Har Das stayed back and the office of *tasbirdar* was created by the Raja of Garhwal for them. The family sustained as painters with eight more successors: Hira Lal, Mangat Ram, Mola Ram, Jwala Ram, Jwala Ram, Tej Ram, Balak Ram, Baiij Nath. Mola Ram remains the foremost proponent of the school but in the absence of patronage post 1812, his descendants became silversmiths.

By 1815, accomplished amateur artists like Baille Fraser made sketches of Gangotri, printed in *Views of the Himachal Mountains* in 1820. These highly embellished prints depict palm trees growing at Gangotri. Perhaps due to the fact that the sketches were cut in lithographs in England, and the printer decided to make the bleak scene a bit brighter!

Then we have Simpson, a professional landscape artist who was in India between 1859 and 1862. In the course of his travels he visited the Gaumukh glacier, the source of the Ganga. He wrote: 'I had my morning dip below the glacier, and I drank a little water.'

I arrived at Gulabrai right after a raging rainstorm blew itself out. The musty scent of the brown earth rose in vapours as sun blazed out once again. I wish I had picked up a *malu* leaf umbrella too! I cursed myself for lack of foresight.

This place is hallowed in the annals of shikar writings, first immortalised in hunter-conservationist

Villages clinging to the calcinated hills

Jim Corbett's *The Man-eater of Rudraprayag*. Of course little remains of the pilgrim-shelters that I had read of as a child, although the spring still gurgles across the highway. A hundred yards beyond, on the left-hand side of the road is a lonely mango tree. This spot is sacred to all Corbett's fans.

Hoarding at Gulabrai celebrates the end of the man-eating leopard of Rudraprayag

In a nutshell, everything is a long saga of ups-and-downs between the years 1918 to 1926, when a leopard hunted animals and human prey as if with magical impunity. It killed 125 people, struck terror into the very hearts of the mountain dwellers, wrecked their daily routine, caused havoc to holy pilgrimages, led to awkward questions in the House of Commons and was hunted by many shikaris. The then princely sum of 10,000 rupees was put on its head as trap-devices, baited goats, cyanide-laced kills multiplied. But to no avail.

Soon, the leopard entered the world of folklore as one in league with the devil. Chaos reigned supreme. Corbett built a *machan* on this very tree, after having worked out that for some strange reason the leopard frequented this very road once every five days. For ten nights he sat up in the *machan* and nothing happened. Then on the dark moonless night of 1 May 1926 the leopard moved in a blurry flash towards the baited goat. A single shot rang out. Then the agonising wait till dawn to follow the trail of blood, to find the man-eater dead, lying in a ditch. With moving compassion, Corbett wrote:

> Here was no fiend, who while watching me through the long night hours, had rocked with silent fiendish laughter at my vain attempts to outwit him.
>
> Here was only an old leopard, who differed from others of his kind in that his muzzle was grey and his lips lacked whiskers; the best-hated and most-feared animal in India.'

As I stand here today, I don't think the self-effacing Corbett would have approved of the garish hoarding put up under the mango tree to commemorate the memory of a man who was lovingly called 'Carpet Sahib'. Out of a time warp in the twilight zone, I come back for a drink from the sparkling waters of the gushing spring, where a boy brings his thirsty cows in. It is a scene that is as eternal as these mountains and shall remain unchanged with the march of time.

Yes! The changing mountains remain unchanged. A bus comes pelting down the road, hits a muddy puddle, splashes water all around. A reminder that we are back on the road to Badri-Kedar. Far below, the Mandakini seems to stand still while the river of many moods, the Alaknanda, booms through the mountains. ●

Mana's Mystic Magic

Winter brings life to a halt in the upper reaches of the mountains

Mana, the last village in the border district of Chamoli-Garhwal, is a place of mystical magic. You are transported to another place, another time, far away... far from the madding crowd. There are just sixty slate-topped houses which are home to some 400 people. The shrine of Badrinath is a mere three kilometres away. Perched on the banks of the mountain torrents of Gupt Ganga and Alaknanda, it is rich in culture, language and believes in equality of all its residents.

Heightened tensions along the Indo-Tibet border have made this place known not only for its rich culture but also its heritage. The people of the Randpa tribe have made Mana their humble abode for generations now, and have settled on either side of the Dhauli and Alaknanada Rivers. The Bhotias who travel extensively along this range have given Mana dwellers the designation of 'Duni Randpa', and those living in the Niti region the designation of 'Niri Randpa'; Randpa meaning dwellers of the valley.

At 10,000 feet, there is not much that one can do. So, the residents turn to business for survival. Mana has always been the hub of activity. But after the 1962 Indo-China war, trade suffered immensely and the villagers had to turn to farming, their sole source of livelihood. One can see the influence of Tibetan culture and language on the people here; their names and religious activities bear a strong resemblance to the Tibetans. In the government records they have been designated as Bhotias and have been given special reservation. A few of them have made it into the army and other posts while the main population is still backward and illiterate.

Closing ceremony at Badrinath Temple

This region is extremely cold, being covered with snow for almost six months in a year. The hills around this place are barren and the villagers have to migrate to warmer valleys of Chamoli and Gopeshwar. The Randpa children study in Mana for six months and the next six months are spent either in Chamoli or Gopeshwar.

At the west end of Mana, is the magnificent Neelkanth peak from which the Alaknanda River

makes its way down to the mountains till it reaches Devprayag and merges into the Bhagirathi. It then flows on to be known as river Ganga in Haridwar. In April and May, when the snow melts, the valley becomes lush green. The soil here is ideal for potato farming. Shepherds inhabit Mana, they spend the night in caves and during the day graze their flocks. The local hooch *changpo* is prepared from barley and wheat in every house in the village. According to the head priest of the Ghantakarn Temple in the heart of the village, 'The liquor is part of the gifts bestowed to please the gods.'

The women of the village are hardworking and intrepid. They keep themselves busy weaving woolens such as shawls, carpets and heavy blankets. The treasures of nature inspire the motifs of the woven cloth. The cloth that is made by the young girls of Mana clad the god and goddess of the Badrinath Temple. A *mangal* song is sung and prayers are offered before the weaving of the the garments begins.

The people from this village call themselves *dobasa*. This means people who dwell in two places. The villagers here wear loose pajamas, shirts, and a cap. They have a custom of wearing a high turban too.

The narrow lanes of Badrinath are a traveller's delight

This implies that in the grand old days of Garhwal, this particular headdress was worn. The use of woolen *kamarbandh* is also part of their wardrobe.

But in today's modern age, the young boys of Mana prefer to wear jeans and fancy jackets instead. The women too have an exclusive dress sense here; such as long *phirans* which are red and black in colour. And *kamarbandhs* are a must.

Mana is also known for its rich herbs. You can smell the bewitching aroma of wildflowers up here. One of the most famous yet rarest herb found in the hills is the *khoya*. The leaves of this particular plant are eaten to cure stomach ailments. Another herb is *balchadi*. The root of a *pip* plant is said to cure stomach ailments too. A tea that is made with *pakhaan jadi*, mixed with salt and clarified butter, if drunk, helps in curing stones.

The young girls of Mana were not sent to school, as their parents didn't think it was necessary. But as time passed by, they realised how important it was for their daughters. There is a strong patriarchal foundation here, but women are given equal rights as well. The oldest lady is the queen of the house. In all festivals and celebrations, the woman is given foremost importance.

Hardworking and resilient, women form the backbone of the economy in the hills

There are many picturesque views from Mana, pilgrims who come to Badrinath visit these places. The famous Ganesh Cave and the Vyas Cave are a must-see. These caves are of great significance, it might be the place where Vyas composed the Puranas and Ganesh helped him in this mighty work. A path leads across to Bheem Pul, it is said that this bridge was constructed by the Pandava brother Bheem to enable his brothers to cross the Saraswati River to the base of the Vasudhara Falls.

Another four kilometers from here is Vasudhara Falls. This cascade falls at least 400 feet to the ground. It looks as if pearls are being showered from heaven. Special permits are required from the district magistrate should the urge to go trekking creep upon you. ●

Looking Down at the Doon

Polluting instudtries like these in the Doon Valley were banned by the the Supreme Court in 1970s

If you look up from your perch in Mussoorie or Landour, the night does have 'a thousand eyes'. But should you gaze at the valley below, a million stars lie scattered down below. When I mentioned this to my old friend, Sudhakar Misra, he, with his matter-of-fact farmer's attitude, quipped: 'Looks more like fields of electric bulbs ready to harvest!' Who could argue with that?

As usual, Misra*ji* always has it right!

It was this vista that my father fell in love with in the 1920s. He had made his way here, from our village in the remote hills of Chamoli-Garhwal, joining the male exodus from the hills in search of a job. At the Rishikesh bus stand stood a strapping sixteen-year old, with little more than his dreams, deciding where to go next. And years later he would remember: 'I had no money, so I looked for the cheapest ticket. Dehradun and Mussoorie won the prize!' This was the beginning of the story of my family in the hills. Years later, I too stood at the same crossroad, but I hung on like a mollusc.

Why you wonder?

Well! I simply forgot to go away!

And living next to Dehra, one is a part of the only district in India whose boundaries are more famous than the district itself. Bounded to the north by the towering Himalaya, to south lay the ancient Siwalik ranges, while to the east gently flows the Ganga and to the west broods her dark sister, the Yamuna.

We are told that countless ages ago, this forty-five-mile long and fifteen-mile wide valley was an immense freshwater lake. On its edges roamed pre-historic life forms—large dinosaurs: the iguanodon; the woolly mammoth, weighing over 2,000 pounds with ten-foot tusks; hippopotami; dinosaur gobbling crocodiles; saber-toothed tiger; and three-toed ancestor of the horse. Their fossilised bones are on display in the Indian Museum in

The arrival of Dehra Dun Railways in 1899 made the hills more accessible to the plains of India

The Dehra Dun Railway was operated by the Oudh and Rohilkhand Railway or the O & R line at the turn of the 19th century

Calcutta. These were excavated in the Siwaliks in the middle of the nineteenth century by Dr Falconer, Sir Proby Cautley, Lieutenants Baker and Durand. Few remember that Cautley was a devoted crypto-paleontologist. Today he is better-known for building the Ganga Canal in the Doab. Whatever happened to that great lake with its dinosaurs?

Among the other legends associated with this fertile valley, my favourite has the sage Kashyapa preparing a great feast for the gods. Indra, the god of rain, was on his way there when he stumbled upon a group of 60,000 pygmies trying in vain to cross a cow's hoof print filled with water—to them a vast lake—Indra found this funny and scoffed at them. Offended, the indignant pygmies decided on revenge. Immersing themselves in austerities, mortification and penance they strove to unseat the arrogant Rain God. Sweat flowed from their tiny bodies and a river was born—known at first as the Sobhan, 'The Pleasant Waters', and in our times, the Suswa.

But the swashbuckling Hyder Jung Hearsey was no pygmy. His descendants insist that he was diddled by the East India Company of what was his rightful purchase of the Doon from Raja Sudarshan Shah. We also remember him as the first person of European descent to actually see the Himalayan ranges from that famous bend near Lal Tibba in Landour.

Dehra was also the headquarters of the Great Trigonometrical Survey of India. It was here, in the 1860s, that Colonel Montgomerie trained his hand-picked native explorers in ingenious secret surveying techniques and then unleashed them into forbidden and hitherto unmapped parts of Central Asia. In these workshops were crafted 'special' Buddhist prayer-wheels, pilgrims' staves to conceal compasses, notebooks and thermometers. The old pundits' haunts evoke memories of Nain Singh, Kishen Singh and Kintup—remarkable men who risked their lives to map unchartered lands.

In more modern times, if you could call 1676 that, the Sikh Guru Ram Rai arrived at the court of Raja Fateh Shah of Garhwal with an imperial *firman* from the Mughal Emperor Aurangzeb and settled in the village of Kharbara, building his Gurdwara in 1699 in the adjoining village of Dhamawala.

Down the ages, Doon picked up a reputation as the 'city of grey hair and green hedges,' where every bungalow, in more idyllic times, had a garden in front, an orchard at the back and a hedge wrapped around it. Of course more than water has flowed down the Ganga and Yamuna rivers since then. Just take Astley Hall, today's plush shopping place, which was once home to the English freebooter Pahari Wilson. Its 300 acres had a stream running across it and was rented, one season, to the viceroy, Lord Dufferin. Even up to the late 1940s and the early 50s, there was Phillip Ryper (a nephew of A.R. Gill, author of *Valley of the Doon* in 1952), who single-handedly turned the Doon Cemetery into a beautiful garden. Lamentably, the gardens and hedges have vanished, gone are the litchi orchards, leaving in their stead a clutter of concrete buildings.

You don't need a genius to tell you that Dehra has changed! If G.R.C. Williams, Assistant Superintendent of the Doon and author of *Memoir of the Doon*, published in1874, were to go through the town now, he'd throw a fit! A population of 66,299 in 1865 has shot up to over eight lakhs today!

But there is something to be said in defence of our early bureaucrats! What began with collecting facts and figures in 1871, after many transfers and

Catching wild elephants in Dehra Dun near Mussourie

A memorial service at Taylor's Flat at the passing away of King Edward

postings, was completed in a little over a hundred days by Williams!

The Gurkhas ruled over the Garhwal and Kumaon regions from 1798–1815 and were indirectly the reason why the not-so-honourable John Company found a foothold in the northern areas. Foremost among the new rulers was Frederick Young, a fifteen-year-old ensign. As a captain, he was A.D.C. to General George Gillespie and was to serve in India for forty-four years in various capacities. As Commandant of the Doon, he took time off from his duties to chase shikar in the foothills. He liked the place and helped set up a Convalescent Depot near Sisters Bazaar, a shooting lodge for himself, and for the spiritual needs of his soldiers, the St. Paul's Church at Char Dukan.

Atop the ridges came the schools. For by 1835, Mussoorie had acquired quite a reputation as a centre for Western education. Some, like the Wynberg-Allen School, established in 1888, were for orphaned Anglo-Indians or children of parents who were too poor to send their children home; others like the Convent of Jesus & Mary, Waverley for girls began in 1845, and the Patrician Brothers' St. George's College in 1856.

Despite all these schools or maybe because of them, naughty Mussoorie has always had a risqué reputation. While her cousins, Simla and Nainital were home to officialdom, the glorified babus were always a bit stiff, because you had the funny feeling that the viceroy was looking over your shoulder. Not in Mussoorie though, people left you alone here and did not bother you. They still don't!

The Writers' Bar celebrates writers who came to this watering hole

The hill station at the turn of the nineteenth century

Of course schools too had their fair quota of scandals, which got hushed up most of the time. The gossip invariably involved rakes and vamps, grass widows and bored housewives. Of which, perhaps, this anonymous doggerel in the *Civil and Military Gazette* holds a mirror to the age:

I had a little husband
Who gave me all his pay
I left him for Mussoorie
A hundred miles away,
I dragged my little husband's name
Through heaps of social mire,
And joined him in November
As good as you'd desire.

By 1900, Mussoorie seemed to have been deemed a suitable residence for native princes. The Maharaja of Kapurthala lived in the lavish Chateau Kapurthala, and the Maharaja of Nepal's Fairlawn Palace was the largest house in the station. Other maharajas included those from Patiala, Jind, Rajpipla, Panna, Baroda, Nabha, and Alwar. There were also the rulers of Tikari, Cooch Behar, Palanpur and Indore. Around this time, the special aura of the hills began to evaporate. Troubles began to plague its schools. In 1900, Mussoorie Boys' School closed its doors due to financial reasons. The dip in the graph took a temporary upward turn of fortunes with the outbreak of World War I.

After such heights, came the fall. The 1934 *Dehradun Gazetteer* says it all: 'Mussoorie has considerably declined in prosperity since 1920 owing to the great decrease in the number of Europeans who visit it or make it a place for retirement. Many houses lie vacant every season and, except in May and September, the hotels are usually half-empty.'

Between 1921 and 1931, Mussoorie's population fell a precipitous 40 per cent. Rescue was around the corner with the arrival of the professional classes: doctors, school teachers, students, small landlords and successful businessmen, who stepped in to fill the vacuum left by the British. They bought their properties, they moved into their cottages, enrolled their children into the cash-starved schools, and predictably, soon the entire hill station was theirs.

The glory of old English bungalows has not diminished with the passage of almost two hundred years

The gathering clouds of World War II brought a brief respite, a sort of last flicker of the lamp before it was finally snuffed out by the depression of 1950s. With the burgeoning middle class joining the fray, business picked up again. Today things have come to such a pass that an old-timer complained: 'This is no longer a hill station. It's become a *hotel* station!' The same was true as early as 1900, when the opening of the Haridwar-Dehradun Railway in 1900 made Mussoorie 'perhaps the most accessible hill station in northern India.' And this cycle is complete now as zippy cars bring you here in just less than six hours from Delhi!

Foremost among Mussoorie's historians was H.C. Williams, editor of the Mafasilite Press, who, as the anonymous 'Rambler', authored the gossipy *Mussoorie Miscellany*. Its doggerel, classic understatement and tongue-in-the-cheek style evokes nostalgia for those days of wine and roses. Of course they were brief, but they linger in the memory years afterwards like fragrance from shattered vases.

Another thing that Mussoorie was rich in was the tradition of local newspapers. It dates back to 1842, when Mackinnon the brewer started the rag chase with the publication of *The Hills*. Five years later, *The Mussoorie Exchange Advertiser* made an appearance, but its only contribution was that the name 'Masuri' was snuffed out to be replaced by the modern 'Mussoorie'. Don't ask me why! Your guess would be as good as mine. But Australian-born writer-barrister John Lang, who died in the hill station, is now something of a local icon for having defended in court, the Rani of Jhansi against the East India Company. Author of *Too Clever by Half*, in about 1845 started a clever, free and easy newspaper under the name of *Mofussilite,* at Meerut, that endured for many years. This gifted wordsmith gives us a mirror image of this pleasure capital of the Raj. If he were to walk down the dusty Tehri road today, he'd feel like a pin in a bowling alley as flashy cars hurtle past him!

'Like meat, we *keep* better in the hills,' wrote Emily Eden in *Up the Country*. True! But not in the winter though. I remember that right up to the 1960s, older folk from the hills would board up their homes in November to spend the winter in the valley down below. Our neighbour, Mrs Edith Walsh ran a guest house at Wolfsburn, her cottage in Landour; she'd head down every winter leaving the place in the care of her loyal caretaker Kalyan Singh. One year, on a cold winter's night, aged ninety years, she quietly slipped away to the land of eternal rainbows. That should have been the end of that one. Or so we thought! Till one night, the chowkidar, dusty, crumpled, dishevelled, pale as a sheet, almost knocked our door down at daybreak.

'Saili Sahib! Saili Sahib!' the words tumbled out of his mouth, jostling and bumping into one another in a frantic haste to get spoken. Breathlessly, he stuttered to my father: '*She's* back! It's March and *she's* back! Walsh Memsahib kept me up all of last night!' Apparently, she rattled the old chain on the hasp and staple of the outhouse door! She kept screeching: 'Kalyan Singh *darwaza kholo*!' Of course we never saw the old chowkidar again. Kalyan Singh was taking no chances. Before the day was out, he had left in a hurry, breathing fear instead of air, for his remote village home. And vanished forever into the mountains!

An image of the old hand-pulled rickshaws that were phased out in the 1970s

The Library Bazaar as it was in the early nineteenth century

North of the Doon valley lies Rajpur, the town that Time forgot. This backwater was once a thriving community of hoteliers: full of wine, roses and song. At the turn of the century, the motor road went past it. Time, that old tyrant, went past, leaving behind memories of better days: decaying bungalows with silent arches, dilapidated *biwikhanas,* mouldering staircases or lonely peepul trees. Fled is the gaiety, gone the merry laughter up the road snaking through the *sal* forest like a monster leaving behind leaves in the Devil's purse.

Tales of long ago are now a part the past; the years sieved by have left a trail of ruin. The reign of the locusts did not exist when the East Indian Railway had got only as far as Ghaziabad. Then, the *dak ghari* was the only means of getting any further. The train arrived in the evening, and if you pre-engaged the *dak ghari,* made your bed there, stowing the small luggage in the 'well' and the larger packages on top; and after dinner made a move.

If you revisit the past, the start was often protracted. A traveller tells us:

> *Dak ghari* ponies are extraordinary animals: they jib: rush off across the road for the ditch; back; turn around and apparently try to get into the *ghari* with you. When, after the *balgir* (as they called the syce) aided by many bystanders, had nearly tugged their heads off; had shoved forward the wheels till the *ghari* propelled the ponies; and the coachman had exhausted every possible opprobrious epithet—the animals would at last, start with a violent jerk that bumped your head violently against the nearest

> panel. Yet broken heads or broken harness, there was no thought of stopping the ponies, once they got going; it was a wild gallop till we reached the next *chowki.*

Though the omnibus was a bigger lumbering vehicle that carried six passengers, it could be tricky, warns our unknown correspondent in 1844:

> When three or four people were lying down, as if in one big field bed, it was well to know something about your fellow passengers. With the jolting of the road, and the eccentric performances of the omnibus starting a 'four in hand', you were apt to get 'mixed up' a bit, and find yourself in someone else's bed, with a promiscuous stranger lying on your chest. Indeed, a trip through the Sivaliks over the pass to Rajpur was an exhilarating experience in the good old days.

Torches and tom-toms accompanying you, by night or day, enhanced the pleasures of the trip. These would scare off inquisitive wild elephants and other wandering and occasional ferocious fauna, which sometimes put a good deal of gratuitous excitement into the journey. There were tales of terror of *mast* elephants resenting the curious lumbering animal advancing on four revolving legs, trumpeting challenges while the terror-stricken coachman vainly extorted dreadful sounds from his bugle. The result was usually disaster.

At the Dehra Bazaar, a change of horses helped in the ride up to Rajpur at the foot of the hills. It was a small place in those days of yore: the houses, each enclosed in a garden or a well-wooded compound, and the green lanes bordered with hedges of roses or other shrubs or trees giving a homely appearance to each house. Rajpur was a thriving town, full of the good things of life: the Prince of Wales' Hotel, the Agency Hotel and some others awaited your choice. You were bound to have no trouble at all, provided you paid your bill.

The hour of cow-dust at Agora near Uttarkashi

The pony ride from here to the hills, on a bright spring morning, was something worth the tedious journey across the flat plains. Walking up the ridge, you find the forest is not dense but changes in character as we climb, the lower part covered with dwarf trees and bushes festooned with gigantic creepers. On the Rajpur side, the trees are stunted; on the other side, the northern, you come upon fine oak and rhododendron trees, not the shrubs you'd imagine, but real forest trees. Ahead, the wild flowers bloom in profusion. The wild pear and the raspberry bushes have managed to survive the scourge of the builders' concrete. Yes! The place retains a charm all of its own.

In 1838, Lady Fanny Eden was delighted with the place which reminded her of Switzerland. Her party went to the hotel run by Mrs Theodore to see her collection of stuffed birds and beasts. Later, she went down the hill attracted by the sound of water cascading down over some watermills.

Don't go looking for them now. They are all gone. The water has vanished. You must remember to thank the reckless quarriers whose rapacious instincts have left cancerous scars on the face of the once-green hills.

'Take your town elsewhere!' One of them said, adding: 'This is the purest deposit of limestone anywhere in India and we need it to make things—from toothpaste to steel.' Irrefutable logic, till environmental activists like the Friends of the Doon and Save Mussoorie Society stepped in. Fortuitously, the law courts agreed and sent our 'patriotic' miners and their ilk packing. Gradually the green verdure returned.

St. Peter's Church in the Cantonment is our first church from the early 1840s

Rajpur is already nearly 3,000 feet above sea level, from where the real climb to the hills commences. There is a very steep pull up through the steep bazaar, which makes the novice rider feel as if he would inevitably slip back out off and over the pony's tail. The old road at the end of the bazaar has been more or less obliterated, and, in its stead you take a winding and fairly level road to the left of the hill to the old toll bar. It was here that one paid the admission fee to the delights of Mussoorie. The old boards announce a rupee for a porter or coolie, eight annas for a pony.

The *gunth* has a thick, shaggy mane, and a very thick, long tail; the most sure-footed, sagacious animal, he never gets tired, and will go all day up and down the hill; seldom fights; and is never alarmed

when passing the most dangerous places. Give him his head, and he will carry you safely. Horses are dangerous and can often become alarmed.

A tale has it that one of these sturdy animals, by accident, fell down a precipice, and was caught upon an oak tree. There he swung; one struggle would have sent him to the bottom, and to certain death; he never moved. The owner got help and had him moved off the tree to a standing place in the side of the hill. They left him there till next morning, to recover from his fright, and pulled him up to the safety of the road.

The mule is a queer-tempered little fellow, and will always kick if you attempt to show any affection by patting him. It does not matter to him. He has a job and he's always willing to do it. Nevertheless, he is as vicious as he is little. Yet none can argue in the face of his sheer tenacity to keep going, regardless.

The ascent from Rajpur is seven miles up, climbing almost every yard of the way, but the first part of the pull up is much the worst. The gradient is steadily steep, and zigzags up the south face of the hill. In the full blaze of the sun, there are no shady trees to protect you. In the old days, the sight must have been quite something. The return ponies and mules coming rattling down as one climbed slowly and painfully, raising clouds of dust all around. The road levels off in the shade below Oak Grove, the Railway School, and it must have been a relief to arrive at Halfway House at Jharipani, to give the muscles a rest and the parched throat some sustenance with a drink, mild or strong. Outside its gate was an old column, now vanished in a landslide, with the following inscription: 'Sacred to the memory of Sir C. Farrington Bart, Captain of Her Majesty's 35th Regiment, who departed this life on the 28th March 1828.'—just the year after the opening of the Landour Convalescent Depot. Captain Farrington was probably an invalid officer, on his way up to the hills for a change. Probably too ill to stand the hardships of the journey in those primitive days, he simply died.

Bearded haystacks in autumn herald the lean winter months ahead

Walking up the ridge, I almost feel for the men who have yet to enjoy this walk in the foothills. To even the most indifferent, it cannot but be interesting. The lateral valley on the left, with its villages and green fields carved into terraces along the hillsides, the varied hue.

The forest patches, the ridges above me dotted with shimmering mansions, the park-like Doon valley below, its encircling range of low-wooded hills, and the shadowy plains beyond, gave at each turn a newer vision.

Sitting under a large jacaranda, catching my breath, I ask only for a willing suspension of disbelief to come with me to the world of the days gone by ... Bands of porters transporting baggage uphill, sturdy hill men from the interior, with enormous loads strapped to their backs, others from the plains easily identifiable by the loads on their heads ... Some carry single loads, others two, four or half-a-dozen together; and in one large box a pianoforte where twenty-four men grappled for a better hold.

Do not for a moment let this wrecked path have you believe that it was always as deserted as it seems. Look beyond, into the halo of the times gone by when mules, ponies and donkeys loaded with grain, mingled with the throng. Though never more than nine feet wide, with often a dangerous precipice on the one hand, yet there was no confusion, and accidents were really rare. Watch the porters sidle to the edge of the road while the rider invariably remained to the ravine side. Probably, the only difficult thing to pass is a huge grand piano, which

The male exodus leaves behind a trail of desolate homes

when overtaken occupies the entire breadth of the road and one must ride it a little way till it is finally crossed at a wider point.

Shattering our reverie is a group of schoolboys scampering down the decline, their backpacks thumping on their backs. There are no porters: signs of the times of plenty! Is there some hidden want? In the slushy quagmire of tourism, will no one listen to this cry in the wilderness? Can't we repair just some parts of the trail? Of course it can be done for very little cost. For in a single day's walk, one could learn more about our precious environment than all the fancy symposiums and seminars held ritually in wood-panelled halls.

'Big is beautiful!' they tell me. 'Think really big!' The larger the project the more money there will be to be made. A wag said: 'The Public Works Department doesn't deal in retail! They only do *wholesale*!' No wonder the department remains a fuel for a great deal of public anger. For if this is true, this trail can wait a hundred years for a newer age.

Do I hear a lone dog bark in the distance and a nursery rhyme echoes in my ear:

Hark, hark, the dogs do bark,
The beggars have come to town,
Some in rags, and some in tags,
And some in velvet gowns. •

Wanderings Around a Hill Station

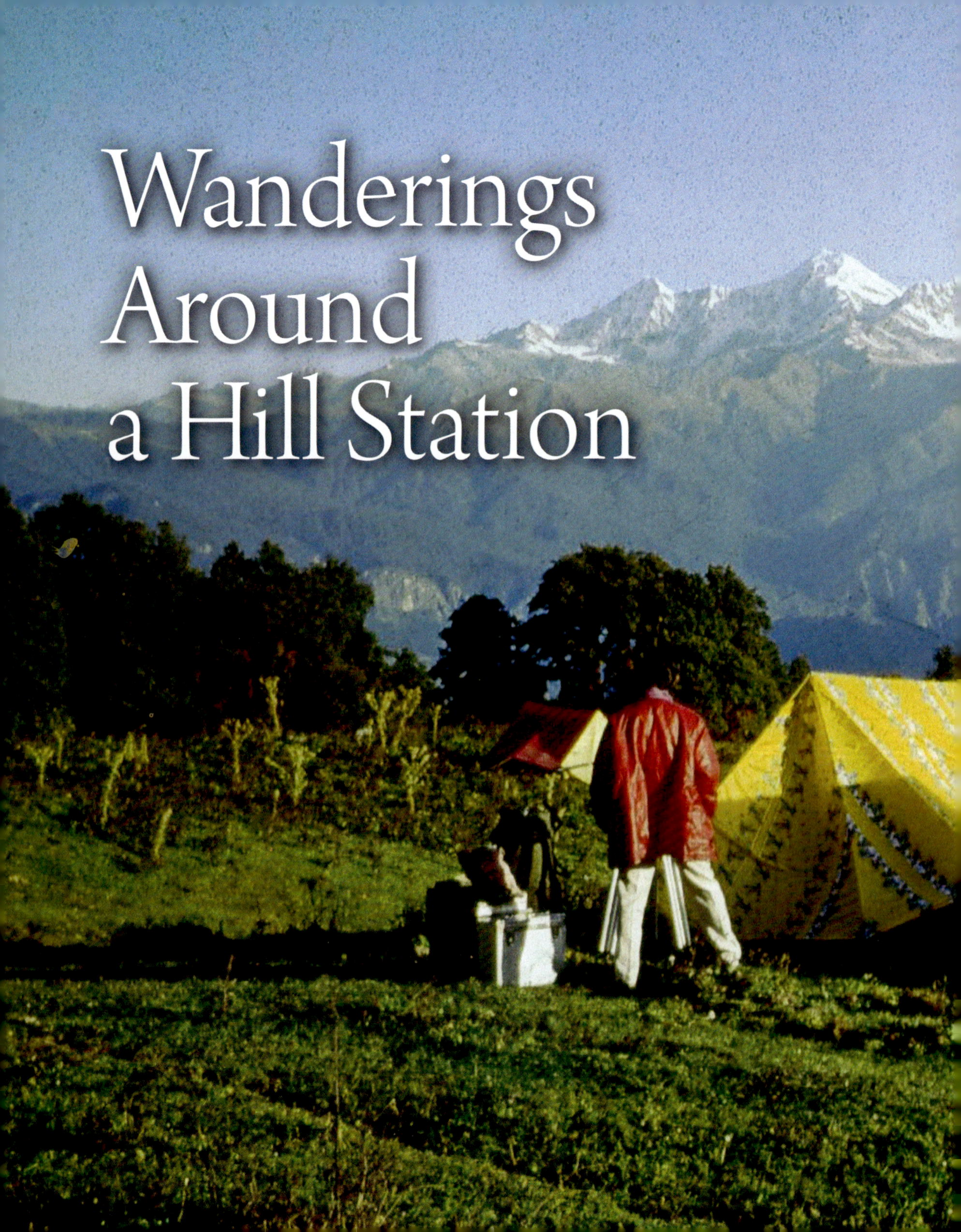

Camping on the meadows

Over the years, like a magpie, our hill peacock, I have collected old maps, trade directories, old postcards, photographs, prints, early guides, journals, newspapers and magazines for tales of Landour and Mussoorie. Rummaging through the drawers of memory, I discover that in my twenties, began this ferreting away of anything 'old' (some of it ephemera) on our home in the hills, till slowly it came to include almost anything I could lay my hands on.

Landour began as a station, a place where the military officers lived in their bungalows and troops in their barracks while the early civilian settlers were invited to acquire estates in the cantonment. Of course there were bound to be others, who preferred the spine of Mussoorie, outside the military area. In our times, Landour is home to merchants, traders, writers, poets, artists, actors, faith healers and antique dealers.

Mountain magic welcomes autumn in the mountains

Perhaps it is opportune to share some of these images with you. Come to think of it, if we were to take them all together in one single embrace, they have never been between the same two covers—ever! You'll find that I have pushed the great wanderer Fanny Parkes together with the maverick, barrister-author John Lang. What do they all have in common? You may fondly ask. They have all come up these hills, at some point in time; they were all great observers and have all left behind word-pictures of the station in the days of its infancy.

I saw my first copy of Fanny Parke's *Wanderings of a Pilgrim in Search of the Picturesque* through a chance meeting with the quiet, reclusive Esther Chauna. On retiring from the British Council Library, she'd winter down in Dehra and in summer, come up to Mussoorie's YWCA. In the late 1960s, old Macquarie Cottage (where the 'Y' was then housed), sat along the path to my college where I'd find her under the shade of a large magnolia tree, editing and annotating these bulky journals. Much later, her Indian publishers for some inexplicable reason decided to publish it from

Karachi! So if you're lucky, you might chance upon a copy of her book.

Parkes' earthy sketches without any frills give us one of the earliest records of life in the station. A difference you will find accentuated when juxtaposed against the British stiff-upper-lip diaries of Lady Emily Eden and Fanny Eden, sisters of the first Governor General to visit the Doon. Of course, for them, the good old *bundobust* took care of it all. My Hobson-Jobson has an interesting entry:

> 'There must be *bahut achch'ha bandobust* (i.e. very good order or discipline) in your country,' said an aged Khansama.
>
> When I have gone to the Sandheads to meet a young gentleman from Bilayat, if I gave him a cup of tea, 'tanki tanki', said he.
>
> Three months afterwards this, well, all changed; bad language, violence, no more tanki.

One thing is certain, Lady Emily Eden never really took to the presence of another Englishwoman in the vicinity, and she looked down her nose as she wrote:

> We are rather oppressed just now by a lady, Mrs. Parkes, who insists on belonging to our camp ... She has entirely succeeded in proving that the Governor-General's power is but a name ... The Magistrate of one station always travels on with us to the next. To each of these magistrates she has severally attached herself, every successive one declaring they will have nothing to do with her ... and the next morning there she is, on the march, her fresh victim driving her in a tilbury and her tent pitched close to his ... Yesterday G. said: 'Here come Macintosh and Colvin on an elephant; how fat Colvin grows! Colvin turned out to be Mrs. Parkes in a man's hat and riding habit. She had met Captain Macintosh and, as far as we can make out, climbed up the elephant's tail into his howdah when least expected.
>
> She will certainly be the death of us all.

Death has not vanquished the writers of the three oldest guides to our town. They defy Time, standing on their own, solid as the old sandstone milestones along the old bridle path from Rajpur to Mussoorie. To my utter surprise, I found all these writers together, meeting one last time at the Lodge Dalhousie (or least their names met) on the same board, up on the wall, under the Roll of Worshipful Masters: John Northam (1870), F. Bodycot (1900) and F. Wilson (1936).

Luckily for the discerning reader, the ever-generous antiquarian Hugh Rayner, publisher of Pagoda Tree Press, reprinted John Northam's *Guide to Mansuri, Landour, Dehra Dun and the Hills North of Dehra,* 1884. Thank you Hugh for ensuring that *this* one sees the light of day!

Shepherds move their flocks to the warmer climes as winter begins

You may glean some of the station's history from compulsive diarists like Mauger Fitzhugh Monk, who was a teacher at Mackinnon's Mussoorie Seminary, our first school, established at the end of the 1830s in Lyndale Estate. They were just letter writers who have left us tidbits of their times.

Other travel writers like Lowell Thomas, in *The Land of the Black Pagoda* (1936) gave us that memorable quote: 'There is a hotel in Mussoorie where they ring a separation bell at dawn so that the pious may say their prayers and the impious go back to their own beds!' And having said that, for some inexplicable reason, he doesn't find much else to say about our hill station.

Others, like the Nobel Laureate Rudyard Kipling (who we all know was partial to Simla) arrived here in the summer of 1888. Staying in Happy Valley, you would have found him tucked away comfortably in the Charleville Hotel. And all this great writer gives us is just four lines inscribed on a photograph of the front office:

And there were men with a thousand wants,
And women with babes galore
But the dear little angels in Heaven know
That Wutzler never swore.

© Ambika Singh

The skies are afire as dusk descends on the hills

And who on earth was Wutzler? Well! It turns out he was the proprietor of the sprawling hotel, whose foul mouth would send his staff scurrying. In our prosaic times, the hotel is gone and in its stead what remains is a collage of modernistic green-and-white buildings housing the officer trainees of the all-India services at what is now known as the Lal Bahadur Shastri National Academy of Administration.

But Kipling has another Mussoorie connection …

In the early days of the Indian National Movement, the Congress had a number of Anglo-Indians in its ranks, one of whom spoke at its All-India session on 1 January 1889. The *Pioneer* came out with a vitriolic article dismissing the conference as a *kathputli nautch* or a puppet show, mocking the presence of 'a brown sahib who called himself a military Captain.' The man referred to was Captain Andrew Hearsey, closely related to the Skinner family of Barlowganj. Not being able to put up with this nonsense, arming himself with a whip, he travelled all the way to the office of the newspaper in Allahabad. On finding that the reporter was on leave, he proceeded to whip the first person he could get hold on amongst the editorial staff.

Memories of Tibet spill over in these hills

Whybank Castle now gone was home to Col. Barlow.

All hell broke loose. The litigation that followed was widely reported in the vernacular press. Badgering the short-fused captain, the opposing counsel held him responsible for much of the doggerel which had been printed by the press, including the Mussoorie journals. The counsel chose a couplet:

> *'While your fathers were selling caps, coats and breeches,*
> *Our sons were fighting in trenches and ditches.'*

'Do you mean to say,' asked the counsel, 'that while you were fighting, we were selling coats and breeches?' Pat came the reply: 'And caps—Oh! And if anything fits you are welcome to wear it'!

Hearsey was charged with assault and sentenced to a month's imprisonment in Naini jail.

In a letter, Kipling wrote to his friend: 'The Native Press is pointing out with glee that I ought to have been whacked ... '

Perhaps he should have been! But Kipling left India soon after.

Yet there were some, not too unlike me, who would never leave Mussoorie. This perch in the first foothills of the Himalaya has been home to a legion of photographers. The earliest was T. A. Rust's landscapes from the 1860s followed by his son, Julian Rust, in the 'Gay 1920s'. In their footsteps followed the Kinsey Brothers, Doon Studio, Mela Ram & Sons, Bhanu Studio, Bora's studio (whose death-mask of the jeweller Janki Das still adorns his shop in Landour) and Glamour Studio, which is still there opposite Vinod's second-hand shop near the Clock Tower.

In the late 1960s, our city fathers in all their combined wisdom built an aerial ropeway from the Mall Road to the edge of the town's water reservoir at Gun Hill. From atop this windswept flat, the view of the Himalayan ranges was stupendous. No one remembers how it all began, but soon after came the largest congregation—forty shops and more—of *photowallas* in any hill resort in the world. They are all adept at turning your fantasies into reality. They dress eager tourists in outlandish *hilly-girl* dresses or turn them into Chambal dacoits, *a la* Gabbar Singh from the blockbuster Bollywood film *Sholay*—complete with bandolier and gun! Photography had truly moved from the studio to the outdoors!

Post Partition, Thukral Studio in London House near Picture Palace was the Mecca of photographers, both big and small. They made great pictures of school activities in town, and on weekends spent Sunday taking pictures around the Upper Chakkar.

From Bannu in the North-West Frontier Province came Taneja with his Rolicord to leave behind images of the hill folk from the adjoining hills.

Just below Christ Church is Mela Ram & Sons. It was the largest processing lab in town till a bank located there in its stead.

Das Studio near Rialto Cinema has vanished as has Rajpal Studio at Picture Palace. With the advent of colour photography in the 1970s, we had the late Gurmeet Thukral's robust body of work. How we miss you Gurmeet! For your imperishable images and for going away without saying goodbye!

At the turn of the twentieth century, analog switched to digital and I see an explosion of images in our times—the age of the point-and-shoot, even if it's your own foot, has well and truly arrived.

But I have to admit that the Rusts have yet to find their rightful place. Ah! What would one do without their enchanting sepia tones of a time when the bungalows were simply lime and mortar pasted onto four-*anna* bricks, topped with thatch roofs!

Rare picture postcards of the hill station

'Today if you stand still for five minutes, they'll build a hotel around you!' lamented the late Colonel Gerald Powell as I photographed him at Wakefield, his ancestral home in the little village of Barlowganj.

Little did he know how prophetic his words would be! Soon after, he'd sold the place to go back to his children settled in England. The new owners flattened the grand old colonial bungalow and in its stead sprouted a concrete monstrosity. Indeed, how right you were Gerry! Stand still for five minutes and they'll have your beautiful old home looking like the backside of an aircraft hangar!

At times like these, one wants to run away like an early visitor who, swamped by the social hurly-burly, wrote:

> 'One day I took myself to task.
>
> 'You have accepted all these festivities,' I told myself! 'You are engaged for a farewell dinner to Colonel B. tonight, you are asked to come with a good repertoire of songs and musical sketches; tomorrow you are to lunch with Mrs.--, to tea with Mrs.--, to dine at the ---. Are you going to do all these things?
>
> 'No--' replied my alter ego.
>
> 'Well, if it is not a rude question, what are you going to do?'
>
> 'I am going to make a bolt of it.'
>
> This is exactly what I did.'

And sometimes, on the rare occasion, *we* too feel like 'making a bolt of it!'

Or perhaps, on second thought, I better leave the present times to the future social historians of

The Mussoorie Seminary was established in 1834, the first school in what was later to be known as the Ediburgh- In- The- Hills

Landour and Mussoorie. Maybe they shall be better equipped to delve into the dust and grime of today's construction activities. At the time of writing, all around me, new houses, like ugly toadstools, are sprouting in every nook and cranny. The grotesque sight of uprooted trees next to garbage dumps are the only signs of progress.

But take heart, the magic of yore lies hidden today just below the surface of the bizarre concrete jungle which surrounds you. Scratch the surface and our history comes bubbling to the surface.

And who's to tell? For out of this churning a new hill station may well emerge!

Though for the present, I am content to retreat from the chaos into a world of glamour, wine and witchery with the poet who said:

You may break; you may shatter the vase, if you will;
But the scent of the roses will cling to it still. ●

A Tour in the Hills

Tented colonies provide succour to pilgrims and tourists alike

Not till they had reached Halfway House in Jharipani did the old-timers feel really refreshed. At long last the scorching sun and the choking dust of the plains were far behind. The breeze soughing through the pines brought back a flood of nostalgia—it was just like home.

While the hill stations of Mussoorie, Nainital, Ranikhet and Almora came into being around the 1820s, Mussoorie had the advantage of being on an outside spur of the Lesser Himalaya. Situated at the extreme edge, it looks down upon the plains as upon a map. One who has had a fill of the place can descend in an hour to the larger world below. So you have a great sense of freedom to be able to get away from it all.

In the foothills of the mountains, what were, essentially, small settlements, grew into larger townships giving birth to the hill stations. And Mussoorie was not named after some place in the British Isles, people were content to follow the name given by the hill folk to the Mansur shrub (Coriana nepalensis). This hardy bush continues to sprout from places where few self-respecting plants would dare even appear.

The front-office-reception of the Savoy was reminiscent of an early railway station

Summer's peak sees the hordes pouring into this place, often called 'the queen of resorts and the resort of kings'; you could say it is a sort of watering hole for the rich and powerful. At the other end of town are the beautiful palaces of the rajas and maharajas of Baroda, Indore, Kapurthala, Katesar and Kasmanda.

Yearnings for home washed over these hills as many old properties bear eloquent witness to the names of those who built them. These houses, though, have changed hands often but the charm of their older names continue. Take my house for instance, it's simply called Trim Lodge, with Trim Cottage and Trim Ville just below in quick succession on the same spur. The family came here in the 1920s. Of the six of us, I chose to stay on here rather than pursue a more lucrative career in the plains. Old friends often tease me for being a mollusc—for attaching myself and staying on here. Or perhaps, just living in the shadow of the Himalayan ranges is itself a blessing.

Anyway, who or what was this 'Trim'? Try as hard as I would, there was no trace of our mysterious Mr Trim. The records of the Municipal Board kept their musty secrets. Or had I been barking up the wrong tree? Firmly established was the fact that the last owner from overseas was a certain Mr E. H. Cockburn, who left the property to his sister by a

The Mussoorie Library, established in 1843, brings back memories of the hill station in its infancy

Left: From small beginnings, a caterpillar awakens on a chestnut leaf

Right: Mullingar's incarnations include schools and hotels.

will. She died intestate. The property then was vested with the Custodian General, who put it on the auctioneer's block. Mr Cockburn's spruce trees, three in all, outlived it all.

May they continue to prosper!

Our pioneers built houses with whatever could be found locally. And everything seemed so nearby: the lime-kilns of Khattapani for mortar, the timber for beams and rafters from the rhododendron and oak trees, while water came on mules from adjoining springs.

On the large flat above us, is sprawling Mullingar which, despite its ruinous looks, stakes claim to being one of the first buildings to come up here and was lost to Lord Auckland, the Governor General in 1838. Apparently, a dashing Irishman, Captain Young, clambered up the hills to build a shooting lodge, taking time off from raising the Gurkha Battalion in the Doon. His fluency in Gurkhali made him immensely popular with those redoubtable fighters. You're right! Mullingar too was christened after a small town off the Irish coast, from where the captain came and returned to on retiring as a general.

The shooting lodge is gone. Mullingar served as a Convalescent Depot for recuperating soldiers or those who came up on furlough. Its next incarnation saw it become the Philanders Smith Institute for orphaned children before being bought over by a local banker's family. Unfortunately, private banks had the awful habit of crashing with monotonous regularity. Soon, a shoddy hotel sprouted. The hotelier passed on and the squatters moved in with alacrity. Sometimes, or so we are told, on moonless nights a ghostly rider arrives astride a white horse, ties him to the rails of the old grille, snaps to attention

The Kellogg Memorial Church came up in 1903 opposite the Guard House. It is home to the Landour Language School

and Captain or is it Genneral Young waits for the twilight parade to begin.

Undeniable nostalgia must have dogged the footsteps of those early visitors as you will still come across houses with Scottish names: Glenbrook, Gorgehead, Scottsburn and Redburn. Mussoorie was a great place for clubs, fancy fairs and dances. While Simla was an officious sort of place, you came to Mussoorie to get away from it all. For here, under the eaves, lonely bachelors met grass widows whose husbands were still in the plains minding the business of the Empire.

What a bold and naughty place was Mussoorie then is illustrated from a report in the *Statesman* of 22 October 1844:

> Last Sunday sermon was delivered by the Rev. Mr. Hackett, he chose for his text Ekekiel 18th and 2nd verse, 'The fathers have eaten sour grapes and set their children's teeth on edge.' The Right Reverend discoursed upon the 'highly immoral tone of society up here, which it far surpassed any other hill station in the scale of morals; that the ladies and gentleman after attending church went on to a drinking shop, a restaurant adjoining the Library and there indulged freely in pegs, not one but many; that at a Fancy Bazaar held this season, a lady stood up on a chair and offered her kisses to gentlemen at Rs.5/- each. What would they think of such a state of society at home?

His admonition seemed to have very little effect. As late as 1932, at a charity show a lady auctioned a single kiss for 300 rupees! A sad commentary on the inflationary trends of the times. Mercifully, Mussoorie was spared the visits of the viceroy or governor.

Wander downtown and you shall come across places like the Himalaya Club, established in 1841 with a membership of 148. The old guide book tells us:

> There are thirty-two sets of quarters in the Club buildings for bachelors, and in 'the Oaks'—a large house with detached cottages, in a bright, sunny spot, with a lovely view, not far from the Club, there are eight suites for married people, eleven suites in all are reserved for ladies. A 'Strikes' court too is placed at the disposal of members.

Another famous club—the Happy Valley Club—was bought by the brewer Mr V.A. Mackinnon in 1904. It was a very civilised sort of place, replete with a reading room, a library, card rooms and a billiard table. Indeed a very wholesome lifestyle awaited members on a summer's sojourn.

Meanwhile, the Mussoorie Library, a historic edifice at the other end of town, was opened to the public in July 1844. A great place for bookworms but if you had other things in mind, nearby was the Band Stand and the Criterion Restaurant where one could sit and hear the band strumming in the evenings.

Ballroom dancing was the rage. At Stiffles and Hakman's Grand Hotel, special nights were so popular that tables overflowed onto the pavements. Mr Roberts and his wife, a well-known dancing couple—looking like Fred Astaire and Ginger Rogers, movie stars of yesteryears, danced the night away.

In Barlowganj stands Sikander Hall. It has been home to many generations of the Skinner family

What became of our dancing gurus? You might wonder. Well! Mr Roberts went back to Europe after the end of the war, where collecting his shares of war reparations, he died most suddenly, some say at the counter. His widow, once a ravishing beauty, continued to receive the proceeds of this money, living the life of a recluse with a menagerie of pet dogs, died five years ago. Briefly there was the era of boarding houses where guests stayed for two or three months. Hotels were impersonal and expensive. But here it was homelier, you met the other guests and if you came with the family, it was cheaper and there was always a place where the children could play in the garden. Mrs Johnson had a guesthouse as did Mrs Walsh in

Wolfsburn, where the students of the Language School could stay at a lower price.

Then came the slump of the 1940s and early 50s, rents were low and people simply pulled down old houses like Wolfsburn, Parsonage, Hollymount, Baroda House, Frosty Hall, Abbey and Snowdown—all cannibalised for tin and timber. The crumbling walls were of no use.

In the boom of the mid-1980s, new hotels sprouted like matchboxes, on their heels trooped the builders wrecking all from Jharipani to Kempty. Only the cantonment with its 168 colonial bungalows managed to survive the onslaught.

More than sixty years ago, at the time of India's Independence, Mussoorie was the most beautiful hill station in the north. Soon after, up the hill trooped the carpetbaggers, peddling dream homes for a song. A rash of mining and reckless building followed in their wake. The place was reduced to a case study of what can happen to a place without a protecting hand, at the mercy of those who take and give back nothing.

Efforts of concerned groups like the Save Mussoorie Society have borne fruit. The hills are slowly turning green again.

And the legacy continues.

Summer's peak sees the hordes descending upon the hill station of Mussoorie. They quite forget that at the northern end lies quiet Landour, waiting to be discovered. Against a frieze of deodar trees, its residents live close to nature and tend to look down upon Mussoorie as one would upon a spoilt brat. Our *two* Upper Malls are real promenades where you can take a walk under a canopy of oak and deodar trees, to hear the cicadas strike up their shrill sword-on-grindstone symphony.

Up until the 1960s, this remained a sanctuary, a sort of summer headquarters of many Christian missions. Exotic names these old properties bear: Oakville, Bothwell Bank, The Firs, Shamrock, Rose Bank, Dahlia Bank, ZigZag, Prospect Lodge, Kilmarnock, Holymount and Ivydene are but a sampling of the names that embellish these old colonial bungalows.

Sixty years after Independence, some of these houses fell into disuse. Many missions were winding up and going home. Some were sold, others grabbed and whatever remained fell into a mission school's share.

At the end of Sisters' Bazaar is Prakash's Store. Famed for its peanut butter with mysterious chunks, relishes, chutneys and jams, it stands as a living testimony to the mysterious power of this cookbook. 'If you can't find it here, you won't get it anywhere!' is the battle cry of their awesome assortment of all you'll ever need. Unfortunately though, with forest fires rampant in the last few years, they haven't been able to make their unique blackberry jam. In a good year, you see crowds of people walking around licking their fingers! No! They haven't been touched by mountain madness! It's just a 'happening year' for the fabled jam. Otherwise do get a nibble of their ripe cheese; you'll become a devotee of their culinary skills. And come back—again and again.

Adjoining Tabor Cottage, a 'boutique' hotel not really ideal for backpackers, is Madan's cowshed—a cure for parched throats at dusk. I once saw a wizened milkman, sitting sobbing. He was really distressed. Was it really *so* vile—the firewater? Or so I thought, until the following exchange set at rest my fond fears:

'What's got into you?' asked Madan.

'I got married to a lovely widow last week,' he explained.

Whimpering almost as an afterthought: 'She's a great cook and washes my clothes too!'

Quaint cottages like these dot the hillsides of the old Cantonment today

'So why the heck are you crying?'

'Because I can't remember *where* I live!' sobbed the old man.

I guess it's that kind of a place. Though, our local brew has nothing to do with Landour's tradition of boarding houses that have seen a recent boom. The demand for accommodation is ever increasing with students flocking to the Language School. So you'll come upon a clutch of guest houses: Rokeby is a three-minute walk from St. Paul's Church; Redburn, two minutes; Deodars, ten minutes; Wolfsburn, six minutes; Bethany, four and Ivy Bank, seven. Understandably, the local authorities had to step in and close down a seedy *sarai* when a guest complained to the owner that his room was infested with rats.

'What time did you get there?' asked the owner.

'Oh! About noon,' replied the guest.

The owner nodded his head understandingly:

'You should go down about one o'clock; they are all in the dining room then!'

Why drag the hassles of civilisation into the hiding places of Nature? Let us roam the forests, ramble over lonely byways until something of the spell of the mountains breaks in on the soul and discloses its secrets.

Carry a picnic hamper brimming with goodies and after partaking of the victuals you'll be one with the Transcendentalists, and hear yourself feeling that

'in Nature's book, no bird, no bug, no bud,
should be forgotten on his day and hour.'

Find yourself a cozy nook, a glade, and a knoll—for this cantonment spreads over some 1,070 acres with just seventy-eight houses. Its quaint bazaar has 300 shops where you'll find the ingredients for your cakes, dealers in fruit and vegetables, grain merchants, and traders of all shapes and sizes.

Walking up the Mullingar slope, you arrive at St. Paul's Church—smack in the middle of Landour. Southward and below lie a group of houses and three or four barracks, some more private houses, the Roman Catholic Chapel of St. Peter's, the two cemeteries and Childers Castle, lodge and cottages, beyond the cantonment's northern boundary. Eastward lies Lal Tibba, more barracks, more private

The pristine resort of Cloud End as seen from Benog

houses and, towards the eastern boundary, the Institute of Technology Management. The highest point in Landour is the Roman Catholic Chapel, 7,850 feet above sea level; Lal Tibba is at 7,464 feet; and both of these tower some 1,500 feet over the highest points in Mussoorie.

The large open flat near the Church has a small park, flanked by the famous *Char Dukan* or literally four shops: Bipin's TipTop teashop, Anil's Café, a post office, a bank, and the Himgiri STD booth. Egg freaks can have a fill of cheese-filled omelettes or try out some of the savoury french-fries. They're crisp and fresh. Highly recommended.

If you take a left, crossing a sturdy bridge, you are at the commencement of the Landour Mall, or western Circular Road, a very pleasant road, running northward under Wolfsburn, past Shamrock towards the entrance of St. Asaph's. Then it turns back along the northeast face of the hill, between the two cemeteries, under the Language School to the Ellangowan junction, from where it goes back to the Church under Rokeby.

Wafted by the breeze, the lingering fragrance of a chiffon cake assaults the senses, transporting you to another time where someone, somewhere, is eating their cake and having it too!

Remember when you're a mile high in the sky, enveloped by the ambrosial air of the Himalaya, in God's own land, with cakes and ale, there is not much else one can ask for!

If you take a walk down the Mall, the local promenade in Mussoorie, take some time off from the tourist traps, drop out, and stop at Christ Church. And you will witness the unique architecture of these houses of worship. They stand today in tribute to the religious concerns of those early founders of the town. Enter a charmed world where magic woven of sunbeams, with no shadow of annoyance, filters through the splendour of stained glass. In a minute, things transform from the ordinary to extraordinary, bringing back a wash of nostalgia—the chimes of the church organ, the peals of bells calling out the devout. Ah! Those days of innocence! When Time waited and the Sandman was banished to tomorrow.

The eternal snows of the permanent snowline as seen from Landour

By 1835 the European population was large enough to warrant the building of a Church. Foremost among these luminaries was George Everest, for whom fame was still far away. Soon the residents settled for a site on a hump above Kulri. Objections came from Mr Mackinnon, then the owner of the first school Mussoorie Seminary, and later a brewery, already a leading man in the hill station owing to his energy and public spirit. Because of the distance from his school, he proposed that the Church of England should be erected to the west of the station. A compromise was effected and the site just above the Mall was chosen. Captain Rennie Taylor, of the Bengal Engineers, Roorkee, built its tower and nave in 1836. The chancel and transepts were added seventeen years later in 1853, when L.D. Hearsey, son of Hyder, presented the bell we hear to this day.

As you walk through the aisles today, the grace of the tapering windows will take your breath away. Considering their fragility and the moments of fury and violence of the past, it is surprising that so much has survived from our antiquity. Of course, this innovation must have been very popular, but try to imagine the difficulty and the risks involved in transporting such treasures, then worth more than their weight in silver.

Buildings which at the pinnacle of their glory must have been a sight, made people feel that they had had a glimpse of Heaven itself. In these houses of worship, bathed in the mysterious light that filters through thousands of little bits of coloured glass, one suddenly comes face to face with a miracle of rare charm and beauty—light that has finally come alive with the colours of the rainbow. You wonder whether the poets of old must have glimpsed something like these as he wrote:

> *Life like a dome of many-coloured glass*
> *Stains the white radiance of Eternity*
> *Till Death tramples it to fragments.*

Historically, the true art of making stained glass reached its pinnacle in the fourteenth century. Those early Gothic glaziers used coloured pot metal, i.e., glass coloured with metallic oxides while in the melting pot, thus obtaining clear, transparent colours. Also used, were white glass and flash glass (glass to which a thin film of coloured glass had been fused). For defining sharp outlines and details, a brownish paint, grisaille, made of powdered glass and iron oxide, was applied and then fired to fuse with the glass surface. A red-hot iron was often used for cutting the glass to the required pieces and shapes. The pieces were then fitted into channelled lead strips, the strips soldered together at junction points, and the whole, installed in a bracing framework of iron.

No ordinary windows these. They looked as if they had been made of jewels: the glass, of exquisite tints, was used in small fragments of various shapes. At first stained glass glaziers made windows, and they relied on pieces of coloured glass to make a pattern. Painters came in to fill the need for art that the glazier lacked. From mere patterns of glass treated with colour, they became pictures of saints and Bible figures, with all sorts of settings and backgrounds.

In the sixteenth century, designs were painted on glass with enamel paints and then fired. So, like all good things, the real art of colouring glass too was rapidly moving towards self-destruction.

Hope came with the birth of romanticism in the wake of the French Revolution. A Gothic revival saw an awakening in the study of glass and other ancient arts. Men like William Morris and Edward Burne-Jones designed windows of true medieval techniques and spirit. While your humble bottle glass had a greenish or brownish tone, due to the impurities in silica, more sophisticated glass required more skill. The turquoise-blue or turquoise-green was produced by the addition of copper. Also introduced were a number of other improvised colours like Iron-stained green, cobalt blue, iron and antimony together, browns and yellows, manganese-stained amethyst and purple. The fine ruby-red you

An early aquatint of the Guard House near the *Nautch-ghar* in Landour

see today is from gold chloride, a discovery in the seventeenth century credited to Andreas Cassius. The drama of their colours, its rainbow sequence of primaries and secondaries, advancing from violet, which is usually the ground colour, through blue, green, yellow, orange and red.

The black on these windows is from the nineteenth century by which a combination of iron and manganese gave the desired effect. The greenish-yellow came with the use of titanium, red from selenium, purple and blue from nickel, yellowish-green from chromium. As for white glass, also known as milk or milk-and-water glass, tin oxide was the favoured agent.

The art of the glass burner explains, more perfectly than anything else, the art of creating stained glass. For all those who worked with metals like copper, brass, tin, lead and iron relied upon their fiery furnaces for success. On a superficial level, stained glass is just your ordinary windowpane given a touch of colour by adding some metallic oxide or by burning some pigments into the surface of the glass itself. These pieces were put together, much as a jigsaw puzzle, with bands of lead till they had some sort of unity. The effect sought after is that of a mosaic or painting but in reality is quite different from both. For the glass burner depends on the effect created by light as it passes through the varied hues of glass. One cannot use unconnected shades in the unending search to create an atmosphere. And one's restricted canvas—a narrow window.

Jharipani's Mossy Falls was named after a banker, Mr Moss who slipped and fell, giving the falls its name

No hue is quite pure. The violet fall somewhere between lavender and grape-jelly purple. The yellow tilt toward citron or chatreuse, and the green favour dusky terre verte. Their power rests on poetry of smoky, grayed greens and blues. Give them time. They accumulate a force of subtle, drenching emotion.

A stained glass window is much more than just a mosaic of pieces of glass. It is a symphony of colour, a moveable feast for the eyes, a thing of passionate beauty and a joy forever! •

Along the Road to Tehri

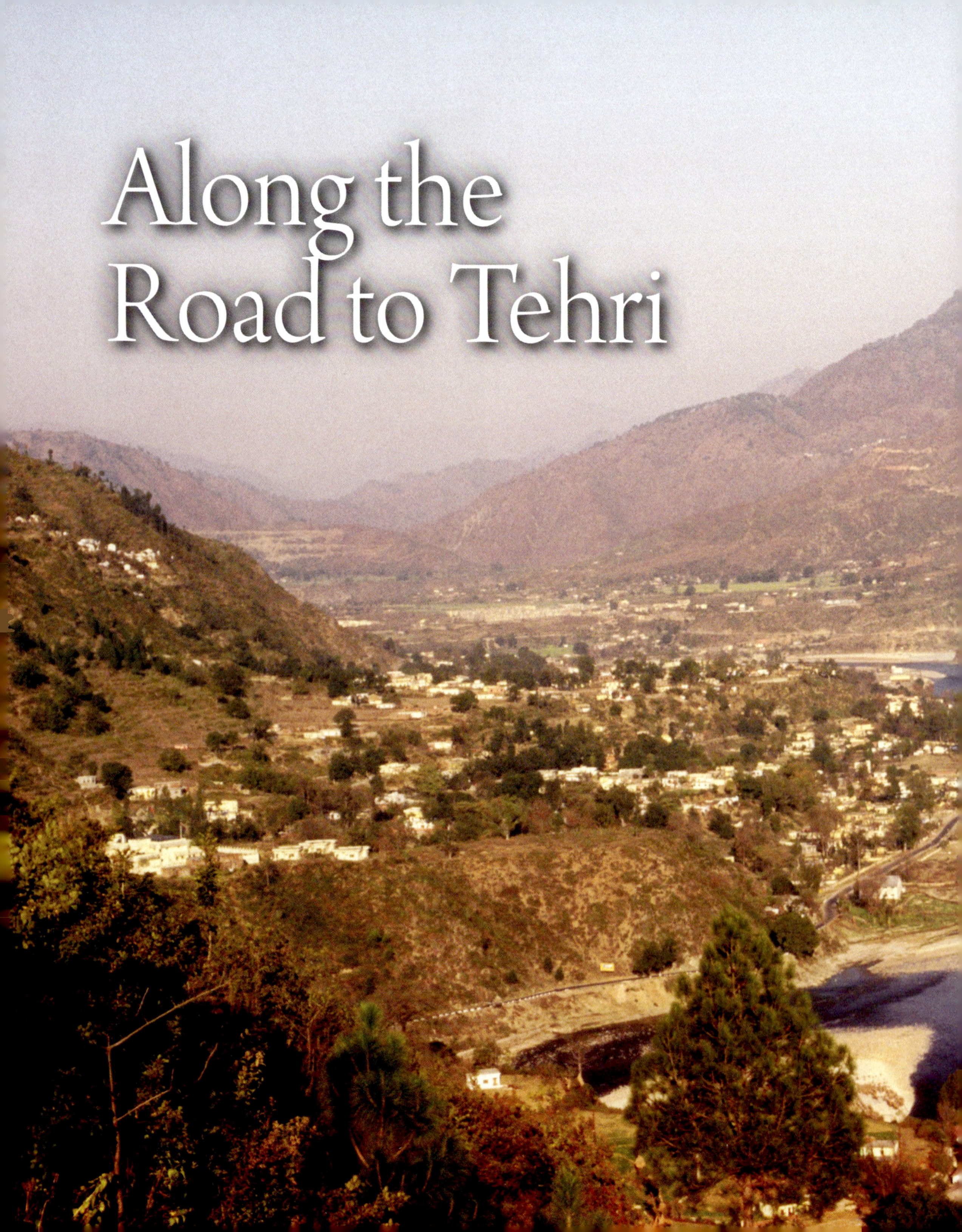

The Srinagar-Garhwal valley is prone to flash floods from times immemorial

I did not take too long to find it. Rummaging through the attic, I came upon a camphor chest. Covered in dust, it was full of the things my grandfather had once held dear. Someone had carefully collected them and put them away from harm's way.

In the coppery shaft of light from the setting sun, I thumbed through a rare copy of Bodycot's *Guide to Mussoorie: With Notes on Adjacent Districts and Routes into the Interior* published by Mafasilite Press in 1907. Scribbled in his familiar hand was a Garhwali Proverb: *'Ek key sair, /Dui koh mela, / teen koh ghapla, /char koh jhamela'*. Simply put, it meant one for a walk, two for a mela, three for a mess and four for a nuisance!

One morning, with a spring in my step, I set out along the road to Tehri. On wheels, you could cover the distance in less than four hours. I was to take three days in the fond hope that it would rub off some of the mud that had stuck to the soul.

Slate-topped homes fill the landscape of Garhwal

Agitations or shutdowns and a fuel shortage had had a salutary effect: vehicles were off the road and I rarely had to jump off the road to make way for a set of speeding wheels. Little has changed here since the turn of the nineteenth century. You could say the road is a little broader and the power lines promise electricity but that's about it.

There is little that you will find on the early rulers of Garhwal. At the end of the Gurkha Wars in 1815, the British laid claim to the eastern portion of the land along the Alaknanda River as war reparations, and left this area to the west to Raja Sudarshan Shah, who died in 1859 without an heir; though in consideration of past services, the Doctrine of Lapse was waived and Bhowani Singh's succession to the throne was confirmed by a *sanad*.

Tehri-Garhwal is spread over an area of 4,180 square miles and despite the clear felling of its forests for timber in the later part of the nineteenth century, the green cover has more or less returned to the valleys of the Bhagirathi and Bhilangana.

In the autumn of 1905, an unknown traveller left us a record of his travels. He must have been a bit 'out of condition' as you find him complaining about the hill folk and their sense of distances:

> The Garhwali will tell you that the march is only 'char kos', which would mean about eight miles or so, and he will point to a spur of the hill in front of you and inform you that the staging-bungalow is just around the spur and in four or five hours you may consider yourself fortunate. Also the comforting assurance about the staging bungalow should be taken with a grain of salt—indeed with a salt cellar full! Only in one thing is he accurate; when he says there is a 'sakht-charhai' you may implicitly believe him.
>
> When the unexpected extra miles that go to make up his 'char kos' and the 'sakht charhai', have both been accomplished you will probably feel completely tired out and hors de combat.

At Jhalki, I had to share quarters with some rather

> odiferous travelers. The camping ground was full of pack ponies, bullocks carrying potatoes, apples and ghee. From the other side, came crowd carrying milk into town. In another part of the ground the export trade was grouped; bales of cloth, grain, kerosene and matches, chiefly on their way to Tehri.

Over a hundred years later, little has changed. Past Jhalki, the houses look like white spots of an irregular pitched camp above terraced fields where the rhododendron, oak and pine have made way for the road.

Dhanualti, our next halt, is twenty-five kilometres but our traveller of old is not convinced: 'It must be an error,' he observes, 'the distance must be so as the crow flies. There are no milestones along the road to guide one, so in the absence of any proof to the contrary we must accept the distance given.' Arriving here, our correspondent goes into shock:

> There is a dwelling house, of sorts, here, approaching in outward appearance (only) that of a European residence, dignified by the name of a staging bungalow. It would defy the skill of the most able architect to define. The remnants of furniture are only fit for a fire-place, and were I a Raja, I would most certainly be ashamed to lay claim to the entire property. Another house is under construction nearby, but it has been in that stage since the year 1898-99 when the designer died and evidently took the plans with him.

Yesterday's bungalow of '*no plans*' is today's Forest Rest House. Though over a hundred years later, it

Sunset hour in the new township of New Tehri

seems so much better than the monstrous concrete hotel that has come up near it. I scurry off down the road to put this ugly tourist trap behind me.

Further down the road, a battalion of pine marches across the well-rounded hills of Chamba. Their long-leafed epaulettes glint blue-green against a dull winter sky. This much maligned tree, finds itself out of favour with environmentalists of the day who fell them to stop forest fires. But they continue to flourish, giving off their own flesh and blood till they wither away spectre-thin and topple over with just a slight gust of wind.

'Nothing ever grows under them,' complains Virendra Singh Kaintura, adding with touching finality, 'and in summer the tinder-dry forest floor catches fire.'

True, those gigantic garlands of fire are strewn across the mountains and refuse to die out till the monsoon drenches the blackened mountains.

Today, a boisterous wind sweeps across Chamba taking on a life of its own: snapping, clawing and tearing at anything in its path. The clumps of pines seem possessed as they sing like a lyre. Then without warning, it abates. Out of the churning dust emerges a scruffy dhaba: a few chairs with the stuffing pouring out of them, a couple of garish sunmica-topped tables and a smoky fire are the only reminders of its days of glory. A signboard proudly proclaims: 'Hilton Hotel: Veg & Non-Veg'. But the coup de grace is in the fine print below it: 'We have no other branches anywhere'.

Apparently, the original owner (for the place has changed innumerable hands over the years) was a baker who came home from

Garhwal Rifles honours its brave sons in Chamba

Dubai, flush with money, and started an eatery. So far ahead of his times was he that the place fell apart. It continues its downward slide much like the road slithering down to Tehri.

Indeed, all that remains of its earlier glory are the faded napkins now being used as dishcloths by its seedy waiters. I'm pretty sure Sir Conrad Hilton would not have been amused!

Chamba is a place with a history; its own niche in the annals of the brave. Its sons rose from humble peasants to peerless warriors in World War I, going off to fight in the distant battlefields of France, where the Garhwal Rifles won three of the five Victoria Crosses awarded to Indians.

Phillip Mason, in *A Matter of Honour* writes:

'They landed at Marseille on October 13th, and on the 29th were in the trenches. Five men were hit the first night during the relief. The trenches were very shallow, hardly deep enough to cover a man kneeling; they started digging at once and having no sand bags, used timber from ruined houses in the villages behind them to improve the trenches. They were always at work on the trenches and every visitor who came congratulated them on what they had done. They had a long spell, twenty days without relief they worked at night, often bare-legged in icy water, to clear ditches and the water away. Twenty years later, at home in Garhwal men showed me feet without toes.

Records have it that on a bitterly cold night of November, Naik Darwan Singh Negi was the foremost in the attack on each successive bay of the trench and although twice wounded in the head and once in the arm, continued fighting till the struggle was over. When his company commander saw him, he was streaming blood from head to foot. His was awarded the second Victoria Cross for an Indian soldier.

Then again, on 10 March 1915, Rifleman Gabar Singh Negi blazed a trail into the history books. His platoon commander being killed, he took command of his platoon. There was a gap between them and the British troops on their left and this section of the trench was full of Germans. Gabar Singh led his platoon to close the gap. The citation of No.1685 Rifleman Gabar Singh Negi, Victoria Cross, of village Manjure, Tehri-Garhwal reads thus:

For most conspicuous bravery on 10th March 1915, at Neuve Chapelle. During our attack on German

St. Paul's Church at Char Dukan is the best restored church in Mussoorie

Bagpipers or *masaks* are a part of the martial tradition in the hills

position, his was one bayonet party with bombs who entered the main trench and was the first man to round each traverse, driving back the enemy until they were eventually forced to surrender. He was killed during the engagement.

Joining the 2/39 Garhwal Rifles at Lansdowne in October 1915, Gabar Singh was only all of nineteen years when he laid down his life, fighting with exceptional gallantry. As the youngest recipient of the Victoria Cross, his valour and sacrifice has been a source of inspiration to all Garhwalis. In Chamba, at the town square stands a memorial to this youthful hero and others from the area. Another VC, Darwan Singh Negi, won the award for conspicuous bravery during the Battle of Festubert on 23 November 1914.

On this day, two Garhwali officers from the 2nd Battalion won the Military Cross, one other rank the Order of British India and two the Indian Order of Merit. Gabar Singh was awarded a posthumous Victoria Cross, the third of the five.

Opposite the Chamba Hilton, surrounded by a clutter of hawkers, is a simple memorial built by men of the Garhwal Rifles to honour these valiant sons of the mountains, who ensured that the Garhwal Rifles remains one of the most decorated infantry regiments of the Indian Army.

The first Royal Battalion moved to a place called Kalundanda in November 1887. The place was renamed Landsdowne in honour of the then viceroy.

During the heady days of the Indian national movement, the struggle for freedom, in the 1930s some battalions of the Royal Garhwal Regiment were disbanded after they refused to open fire on unarmed demonstrators in Peshawar. Some of these brave dissenters went on to join the Indian National Army. Chander Singh 'Garhwali' joined the galaxy of freedom fighters who was sentenced to life for his role in the revolt at Peshawar.

Outside, the roar of a river booms through the rapids. But I know there is no river up here on the ridge. It could only be the wind back again, picking up a storm as it rushes through the arching pines.

Carried by the gust is the skirl of a bagpipe. Narain Das carries his *mashak* (as the bagpipe is called) at the head of a wedding procession. He retired from the army band a long, long time ago but carries with him the music of Scotland, sans the tartan kilt, to the highlands of Garhwal. ●

Index

A

Acchari-geet, 51
Almora, 57
Anjani Sain, Tehri Garhwal, 36–37
Astley Hall, 194
Atkinson, E.T., 14

B

Baadis, 51, 98–103
Badrinath Temple, 15, 41, 121
  closing ceremony at, 186–187
Ballads (songs), 51
Balpa Sulera caves, 76–77
Batten, J.H., 88
Beech marten, 146
Bhagirath (King), 40, 42
Bhagirathi valley, 12
Bhandari, Madho Singh, 15, 172
Bhatt, Chandi Prasad, 169
Bhatwari, 169
Bhyundar Valley, 104–113
Brunton, Paul, 27–28

C

Cautley, P.B., 118
Chamba, 236
Champawat tigress, 31
Chandrashila, 92–97, 161
Char Dukan, 226
Chopta, 161
Churails, 154
Civil and Military Gazette, 197
Coaduwar Gaut, 177
Cobra Lily, 133
Corbett, Jim, 31, 33–34, 183

D

Dak ghari, 200–201
Das, Har, 181
Das, Shaym, 181
de Andrade, Antonio, 11, 176
Dehra Bazaar, 201
Dehradun, 190–205
  arrival of railways in, 192–193
Dehradun Gazetteer (1934), 197
Deodars, 134–135
Deralle village, 84
Devprayag, 68, 78–79, 173
Dhanualti, 234
Dharali, 156–161
Didsari village, 167
Dodital, 46
Doon Valley, 190–205
Drums, and celebrations in hills, 67

Duggalbetta, 95, 158–159
Duirital, 43, 69, 86–91

E

Early Jesuit Travellers in Central Asia, 11
Eden, Emily, 209
Education, in Garhwal, 49
Execlensia pines, 82

F

Feinkamal, 129–130
Flowers, Himalaya, 124–133
Folk-dances, at Wan village, 74–75
Food, in riverine valleys of Garhwal, 48
Four-horned ram, 70–77
Fraser, Baille, 13
Frazer, Baillie, 82

G

Gaikwad, Seema, 169
Gairola, Tara Dutt, 56
Ganesh Cave, Mana, 189
Ganga, at Rishikesh, 14
Gangnani, 82
Gangotri, 20–21
Gangotri Temple, 23, 83, 84, 181
Garhwal, 38–43
  trekking, 44–59
Garhwal Himalaya, 26–27
Garhwali, Chander Singh, 11
Garhwal Paintings (Lal), 51
Garhwal school of painting, 181
Gaumukh glacier, 117
Geyer, William, 76
Ghagharia, 28–29, 104–105, 108, 109
Glaciers, of Uttarakhand, 40
Goatsucker, 146
Gohna Dam tragedy, 175
Govind Ghat, 107, 108
Great Himalaya, 22
Guide to Mussoorie: With Notes on Adjacent Districts and Routes into the Interior, 232
Gunth, 202
Gurkhas, invasion into Garhwal, 57, 82–84
'Gurkhyani,' 101

H

Hamer, Robin, 155
Happy Valley Club, 222
Hardwicke, Thomas, 14
Haridwar, 114–123
  Mughal frontier guards at, 176
Har-ki-Pauri, 116, 123
Hatwal, Rameshwar Dutt, 85
Hedin, Sven, 142
Hemkund, 108, 112
Herdsman, as vocalist, 51
Himalaya Club, 222
Himalayan Folklore (Gairola and Oakley), 56
Himalayan Gazetteer, 36
Hiuen Tsang, 42–43, 120, 167
Hulme, James, 84

J

Jamak village, 167, 169
Jayal, Narendra Dhar, 27

Jhawanu, 177

K

Kakbhushandi Tal, 178–179

Kanwar/kanwarias, 122

Kedarnath Temple, 164–165, 168

Kellogg Memorial Church, 221

Kharsali, 38–39, 154

King Lear, 76

Kipling, Rudyard, 210

Kumbh Mela, Haridwar, 121

Kushkalyani, dry meadows of, 148–149

L

Lakhamandal village, 62, 64–67

Lakshman Jhula, 118–119

Lal, Mukandi, 51

The Land of the Black Pagoda (Thomas), 210

Land of the Gods, 30

Landour, 208

La Prima Catholica Net Tibet, 11

Legge, Joan Margaret, 109

Lesser Himalaya, 22

Library Bazaar, 200

Loharjung, 72

Lokpal, 110

M

Madhmaheswar, 153

Maithani, Gopal Dutt, 97

Mana village, 184–189

  dressing style, 187, 189

  herbs in, 189

  women of, 187

The Man-eater of Rudraprayag (Corbett), 183

Mangal song, 187

Mason, Phillip, 236

A Matter of Honour (Mason), 236

Medical facilities, Garhwal, 48

Memoir of the Doon (Williams), 194

Messner, Reinhold, 27

Momiai, 153–154

Mossy Falls, 229

Mount Kailash, 24

Music, 50–51

Musk deer, 147

Mussoorie, 192, 195–200, 218, 221

  population, 197

The Mussoorie Exchange Advertiser, 198

Mussoorie Library, 219, 222

Mussoorie Seminary, 215

N

Nanda Devi, 34, 35–36, 75

Neel Ganga, 81

Neelkanth peak, 186

Negi, Gabar Singh, 236

Negi, Sumer Singh, 55

Nightjar, 146

Noyce, Wilfred, 26

O

Oakley, E. S., 56

'Ocean of Rocks'—Shailsagar, 43, 77

Ophrysia superciliosa, 145

Oxalis, 128

P

Paintings, 51–52
Panwaras (songs), 51
Paradise flycatcher, 142
'Paradise Ground,' 20
Parasols, as symbol of Nanda Devi, 76
Pari Mandir, 31
Parke, Fanny, 208–209
Pather Nachauni, 76
Peacock orchid, 128
Pica, 142
Purnagiri, 33, 34
Pushpa Ganga, 62–63, 106

Q

Quaint cottages, 224–225

R

Raj Jaat Yatra, 42, 72–77
Rajpur, 200–202
Rajput families, in Himalayan districts, 56
Ram, Mola, 14
Raphael, Cyril, 169
Rhododendrons, 127
Richmond, Hilda, 155
Roopkund, 22, 43, 77, 172
Rudraprayag, 170–171, 175
Ruttledge, Hugh, 35–36
Ryper, Phillip, 194

S

Saili, Ganesh, 17
Scarce, as paintings, 52
Shah, Kirti, 174
Shah, Shyam, 14, 172
Sharma, D. K., 28
Sheep rearing, 83
Sheep sorrel, 128–129
Shipton, Eric, 34
Sikander Hall, 222
Silver rupees, 54
Singh, Chait, 58
Singh, Chattar, 72, 74
Singh, Khem, 110, 113
Singh, Murari, 164
Singh, Thakur Surbir, 11–12
Siwaliks, 22
Smythe, Frank, 15, 26–27, 29, 31, 33–34, 57, 109, 121
St. Paul's Church, 237
St. Peter's Church, 202
Suman, Sridev, 15
Swami Manmathan, 176

T

Talla Des (man-eating tigress), 34
Tehri, 15, 230–238
Tented colony, at Dharali, 156–157
Terai forests, 141
Terray, Lionel, 40
Thalesagar peak, 25, 32–33
Thomas, Lowell, 210
Tillman, Bill, 26
Tilman, H.D., 34
Too Clever by Half, 198
Trekking, 44–59
Tungnath, 8–9, 95, 161

U

Udak-kund, at Kedarnath, 167
Ukhimath, 95
Up the Country (Eden), 199
Uttarkashi, 162–169

V

Valley of Flowers, 26, 106, 130
The Valley of Flowers (Smythe), 15, 57, 109
Vasudhara Falls, 189
Views of the Himachal Mountains, 181
Vyas Cave, Mana, 189

W

Wanderings of a Pilgrim in Search of the Picturesque (Parke), 208
Wan village, 74–75
William, G.R.C., 15
Williams, H.C., 198
Wilson, Pahari, 12, 81, 159–161
Wood sorrel, 128
Writers' Bar, 196

Y

Yamuna, 60–69
Younghusband, Francis, 26